THE

OTHER

SIDE

OF

GROWTH

An Innovator's
Responsibilities
in an
Emerging World

Anthony Mills
Editor

The Other Side of Growth

An Innovator's Responsibilities in an Emerging World

First Edition: 2020

Anthony Mills

Editor

GInI

Copyright © 2020

Global Innovation Institute

Grand Rapids, Michigan, USA

Global Innovation Institute

gini@gini.org

USA

ISBN: 978-1-7351046-2-1

CONTRIBUTORS TO THIS BOOK

The following individuals have each contributed to this book. At the time of this book's writing, each of these individuals actively serves on the Board of Advisors of Global Innovation Institute | GInI (Grand Rapids, Michigan, USA).

Anthony Mills	Global Innovation Institute
Dr. Larry A. Schmitt	The Inovo Group
Dr. Bettina von Stamm	Innovation Leadership Forum
Steve Wells	Legacy Innovation Group
Mick Simonelli	Mick Simonelli
Michael Graber	Southern Growth Studio
Teresa Spangler	PlazaBridge Group
Bryan Mattimore	The Growth Engine
Mike Pinder	Mike Pinder

ABOUT THE CONTRIBUTORS

Anthony Mills is the Executive Director of Global Innovation Institute. He is a globally sought-after thought leader on emerging markets, responsive growth strategies, corporate innovation, business insights, workplace experience, entrepreneurship, product design, and Design Thinking. His work at GInI has had a deeply profound and lasting impact on businesses all over the world.

Anthony is also an award-winning and internationally-recognized innovator, having brought numerous innovations to the companies he has served. He is a deeply associative thinker – a consummate rainmaker – with a classic 'Innovator's DNA' profile. His lifelong disdain for the status quo, and his love for pursuing 'what's next', have garnered him a well-earned reputation as an agent of change. Furthermore, having traveled the world and experienced many cultures up close, he understands people, and with them, the markets they make up. He knows how to combine insight and empathy with imagination and creativity to conceive real solutions to customer's 'deep-down' needs and desires. And he knows how to connect business insights in ways that let companies deliver the winning value propositions and customer experiences they need to truly lead their markets.

Anthony holds graduate degrees in engineering and management from North Carolina State University (Raleigh, NC) and Aquinas College (Grand Rapids, MI).

Dr. Larry A. Schmitt is a Founder and Managing Partner of The Inovo Group, a provider of strategic innovation consulting services. Since co-founding Inovo in 2001, Larry has led their growth to become a successful, recognized leader in the field of innovation.

Larry draws upon years of experience in both large corporations and startups that wrestled with how to innovate. He has worked closely with Inovo's clients including Cargill, Dow Chemical, Honeywell, Corning, United Health Group, ExxonMobil, Saint-Gobain, and DuPont, among many others, all of whom draw upon the frameworks, methods, and tools he and others at Inovo have developed over the years to improve strategic innovation portfolios and capabilities.

Larry regularly writes and speaks on innovation and related topics. He holds a PhD in Computer Science from the University of Wisconsin and a BS from the University of Michigan.

Dr. Bettina von Stamm has been an original and visionary thinker as well as a prolific writer in the field of innovation since 1992.

Her perspective on innovation builds on three foundations:

— The importance of a deep understanding of specific context - reflected in her facilitated assessment tool for innovation conditions, the InnovationWave®.

— The necessity to take a systemic approach - is reflected in her BvS Innovation Framework.

— A deep focus on people - which is supported by two sets of picture cards that help elicit assumptions and bridge chasms so common in the highly diverse contexts that innovation requires.

She captures her approach, means of communication, and effect as follows: Innovation Philosopher, Story Teller, Catalyst.

As the Founder and Director of the Innovation Leadership Forum, Bettina works with leaders and leadership teams to give them confidence to innovate and collaborate in the 21st century. She delivers executive programs at prestigious universities and corporations around the world. Her most recent clients include 3M, Cambridge University, DEUSTO Business School, Glen Dimplex, Imerys Carbon & Graphites, Sanofi Aventis, Siemens and Steelcase.

Following her deep conviction about the importance of sustainability as a key driver for innovation, Bettina joined Katerva, a non-profit whose mission is to identify, evaluate, and accelerate sustainable disruptive innovation, as Director of Awards in Autumn 2015.

She is a Fellow of the German-based Peter Prebilla Foundation, the UK-based RSA (Royal Society for the encouragement of Arts, Manufactures and Commerce), and holds the position of Visiting Professor at Middlesex University. Her prolific writing includes 4 books and innumerable articles. Bettina holds an MBA as well as PhD from London Business School, as well as a first degree in Architecture and Town-planning.

Steve Wells serves as Director of Insights at strategic innovation consulting firm Legacy Innovation Group.

Steve is a seasoned Market Strategist and has worked in this field for many years inside of Fortune 500 businesses.

His work has focused on large-scale market forces, their impact on consumers, and the implications for future strategies. Through this work, Steve has been instrumental in shaping the course of market insights, corporate and brand strategies, product innovations, and sales strategies.

Steve has pursued his passion for understanding how cultural and market changes impact business. As an internal consultant for two Fortune 500 companies, he kept an eye on a wide range of business drivers from the economy to social trends to technologies and everything in between. He was able to identify key shifts the company leveraged to develop products that were right for their customers at the time, which maximized their market success.

Having participated in countless innovation sessions, product and brand development projects, and strategic planning sessions, Steve has a unique perspective on the needs of business and an ability to see how they can identify and act on market opportunities. Steve is a deeply associative thinker – constantly connecting dots to reveal new patterns that businesses leverage for strategic value. He uses this skill, together with his many insights and experiences, to lead clients toward broad market opportunities and clear paths of action. Steve has led countless innovation workshops with Fortune 500 clients that have produced numerous high-impact opportunities.

Steve also holds certification in Strategic Foresight from the University of Houston (Houston, TX) – one of only four schools in the world to offer this certification. This has reinforced Steve's ability to conduct deeply insightful strategic futuring work. Steve also holds a BA in Psychology and Religion from Greenville College, and an MA in Religion from Trinity International University.

Mick Simonelli is an independent consultant and thought leader on innovation in financial services. Previously, Mick served as the senior innovation executive for USAA, where he built and led the innovation program to world class status. During his tenure, USAA received numerous awards and accolades including InfoWeek 500's Most Innovative, Businessweek's #1 Customer Service, and People's Choice Awards. Before that, Mick served as an innovator in multiple positions within the Department of Defense where he helped digitize and transform the US Army.

Mick is a Certified Management Accountant and possesses advanced degrees in Business and Psychology. A natural change agent, Mick is an executive innovation practitioner with his work appearing on NPR, American Banker, Harvard Business Review, Workforce Magazine, Fast Company, and has been the subject of numerous academic articles.

Michael Graber is the Managing Partner and founder of Southern Growth Studio in Memphis, TN. His work inspires and embeds systemic and genuine innovation inside client cultures, both the methods and the mindsets.

Since launching the Studio in 2007, he has helped more than 200 clients embrace a very pragmatic approach to growing market share through innovation, insights, and strategy. Michael publishes and speaks frequently on these topics – and this same passion gets applied when he works with mid-sized companies, global nonprofits, and Fortune 500 businesses.

Michael has more than 25 years of experience leading market strategy and innovation efforts. An expert in experiential marketing and user interface, Michael has consulted across a wide range of industries through his work at iXL, advertising agencies, and as an executive in a high-growth technology company. A published poet and musician, Michael is the creative force that compliments the analytical side of Southern Growth Studio.

Michael holds a MFA from the University of Memphis. Visit www.southerngrowthstudio.com to learn more.

Teresa Spangler has been a driving force behind innovation and growth for more than 30 years. Today, she wears multiple hats as a social entrepreneur, innovation expert, growth strategist, author, and speaker (not to mention mother, wife, band-leader, and so much more). She is especially passionate about helping CEOs understand and value the role human capital plays in innovation, and the impact that innovation has on humanity; in our ever-increasing artificial/cyber world. Teresa shares her insights on these very topics (and more) as a member of the Forbes Technology Council. She is the mastermind behind the GameDay Decisions Analytics Platform™, an integrated artificial intelligence and machine-learning platform as a service to "Simplify the Art and Science of Decision Making."

Throughout her career, she has worked for global brands like Tom Peters Company and Red Hat Software where she held senior executive positions and was responsible for successfully leading revenue growth pre and post IPO. In addition, she has founded and led a number of entrepreneurial organizations through growth milestones including venture capital funding, IPOs, innovation consultancy, and technical services company. She also founded a philanthropic performing arts organization, which created showcase opportunities for more than 200+ original artists and musicians over 7 years that captured the attention of New York dance communities and globally known musicians. She is the author of the book All That I Am Know That I Know: 17 Life Lessons for Entrepreneurs, and of the book series Game of Life. She holds a BS from Appalachian State University and Executive Leadership & Management certifications from Duke University and Harvard University.

Teresa has held many advisory board roles for startups and organizations such as Business Innovation and Growth Council, The Council for Entrepreneurial Development, and The NC World Trade Association. Teresa's passion for the arts and music can be witnessed first-hand when she performs as a singer/songwriter and guitarist as the lead singer of The Headless Chickens.

Bryan Mattimore specializes in ideation and innovation process, front-end marketing research, branding, creating and developing new products and services, and innovation strategic planning.

He is Cofounder and 'Chief Idea Guy' of the Growth Engine Company, a twenty-year old innovation agency based in Westport, Connecticut. Prior to cofounding Growth Engine, he was president of the Mattimore Group, a fifteen-year-old ideation facilitation and creativity consulting company. In his business consulting career, Mr. Mattimore has facilitated over a thousand brainstorming sessions, moderated over five hundred creative focus groups and consumer ethnographies, and managed over two hundred successful innovation projects, leading to over $3 billion in new sales annually for a wide variety of Fortune 500 clients.

Companies that Mr. Mattimore has worked with include: Accenture, AstraZeneca, ATT, Bayer, Black & Decker, BNY Mellon, City of New York, ConEdison, Danaher, Dun & Bradstreet, Eaton, Esselte, Essilor, Ford, Grumman Data Systems, Halliburton, IBM, ITT, Johnson and Johnson, Lexis-Nexis, Lockheed Martin, Lucent, LVMH, Merck, Microsoft, Novartis, Pepsi, Pfizer, Philips, Pitney-Bowes, Procter and Gamble, Shell Chemical, Sony, State Farm, Time-Warner, United Technologies, VSP, and Unilever.

He speaks frequently to organizations and associations on innovation processes best practices. He has addressed or co-chaired conferences for the Industrial Research Institute (IRI), Product Development & Management Association (PDMA), American Marketing Association (AMA), Association of Talent Development (ATD), Vistage, Young President's Organization (YPO), and the World Innovation Forum. He is also an instructor for Caltech in their Executive Education program.

Mr. Mattimore has authored dozens of published articles and webinars, and three books on business creativity and innovation process: 21 Days to a Big Idea, Creating Breakthrough Business Concepts, Idea Stormers, How to Lead and Inspire Creative Breakthroughs, and 99% Inspiration, A Real World Guide to Business Creativity.

A cum laude graduate of Dartmouth College, with a major in psychology, Mr. Mattimore is also the inventor of the creativity training game, Bright Ideas.

Mike Pinder is an expert on innovation. As former Expertise Lead at Board of Innovation, he consults cross-industry in B2B & B2C helping Fortune 500's to innovate like start-ups.

Mike applies a multidisciplinary background spanning innovation strategy, design, business, and innovation management through hands-on consulting, training, and facilitation of tailored innovation programs. He regularly authors thought-leadership pieces and gives international keynotes and lectures on innovation.

Mike guides innovation strategy, designs and runs corporate accelerators, builds long-term cultural transformation programs, and grows strategic innovation partnerships with corporates like: GE, World Economic Forum, AstraZeneca, Logitech, ING Bank, Fazer, AB InBev, Atos, Zeppelin Foundation, and many others.

For more information, visit www.mikepinder.co.uk.

CONTENTS

THE OTHER SIDE

OF

GROWTH

PROLOGUE

Anthony Mills

Introduction

In the Spring of 1972, the Club of Rome published its seminal work <u>The Limits to Growth</u>[1]. This report detailed the findings of an in-depth research and simulation study conducted by an international team at the Massachusetts Institute of Technology into the limits of exponential worldwide growth – including the production and consumption of material goods and the resultant environmental depletion that came with them, given Earth's finite resources. That study concluded that there were, in fact, limits to the exponential industrial-era growth the world was experiencing at the time. Beyond those limits, such unfettered growth would no longer be viable. The study also concluded that the world of that time was moving quickly toward these limits, but that there was hope – a hope that lay in mankind finding an equilibrium anchored in self-imposed limitations.

Now fast forward nearly 50 years. It has become abundantly clear that the world has not only met, but <u>exceeded</u>, the limits defined back in 1972. This has had – and continues to have – significant ramifications for our world, not only environmental ramifications, but just as importantly, societal and economic ramifications – with major implications for who we are, and will continue to be, as a collective humanity. What that study did not anticipate back in 1972 was the powerful forces of <u>innovation</u> that the world would witness over the coming 50 years. Consequently, our world today faces stressors – both positive and negative – that have never before been seen in the course of modern humanity. On the positive side, there have been tremendous advances in medical technology, ubiquitous connectivity through advanced mobile technologies, greater accountability for political leaders due to social media, and so on – many of which have contributed to a massive reduction in global poverty worldwide. But on the negative side, we have catastrophic global climate change, digital addictions, rampant teen suicide, engineered pandemics, and as much racial tension as ever before.

From an innovation and technology standpoint, things have unquestionably gotten better – many activities are now far more streamlined than they were in the past, owing to ongoing digitization of the world, and owing to the fact that we now far better understand what innovation entails, and precisely how to make it happen. Consequently, we have made incredible progress toward achieving a truly 'frictionless economy', and as a result the transactional costs of conducting business have diminished to a fraction of what they once were (making it easier than ever to start up a new business). And in terms of certain measures of global wellbeing, such as the number of people living in extreme poverty, and the overall global fatality rate associated with avoidable diseases, there has likewise continued to be downward trends – a very positive sign. At the same time however, new ills are confronting our world, such that in the grand balance of things, is our world better off than it was 50 years ago?

I believe that most people would agree that, on balance, yes, it is better off than it was 50 years ago. But they would also recognize that as it has gotten better, it has at the same witnessed the incredible negative effects of many of the new innovations that we have introduced. And so our real question in moving forward now is… "How can we – as innovators – better anticipate such negative effects, and then work conscientiously to avert them?"

That is the lead-in question we ask you to ponder as you take in the chapters that follow. Each of these chapters have been written by a global thought leader in the field of business innovation and strategy. These individuals have each put deep thought into this subject, and offer their own unique perspectives on the matter. Together they will enlighten and greatly broaden your perspective – to see beyond growth purely for the sake of growth, and to instead understand a grander vision for this world that we all live in – a vision for a truly better world.

Who Is This Book For?

This book is intended for business leaders – those whose job it is to conceive and execute new strategies on behalf of their business, including innovation, technology, production, and delivery strategies.

What is the Purpose of This Book?

The purpose of this book is to provide the reader with a broad and eclectic set of perspectives into 'the other side of innovation'. This 'dark side of innovation' is the side that openly acknowledges the potentially negative consequences of what we as innovators create, not simply their benefits – however unintended and unforeseen those consequences may be.

For example, in the days before social media, did we foresee cyber bullying and fake news? In the days before internet gaming, did we foresee internet gaming addictions? And in the days before engineered biological weapons, did we foresee the catastrophic economic fall-out of a global pandemic?

The purpose of this book is not to give the reader the answers to any particular situation. Rather it is to suggest to the reader new questions they should be asking of themselves about their own business' strategies and initiatives… questions that perhaps they should have been asking all along but haven't been. Perhaps this was because they did not know the right questions to ask, or how to ask them, or even if they did, what to do about the resultant answers. Or perhaps they were afraid of the answers because there was insufficient organizational support for properly addressing them.

Using these questions, a business leader must construct and contemplate a broad range of future scenarios that could play out, so as to develop strategies that will enable them to shape the future to achieve a more ideal outcome.

Therefore, our challenge to you, the reader, is to begin the process of asking these questions and thinking deeply about the profound implications of the answers you come up with. In particular, our desire is for you as a business leader to thoughtfully reflect on the impacts your strategic decisions will have – including the inevitable unforeseen consequences. We ask you to work through the plausible and important future scenarios that could play out – and then, to devise new strategies that thoughtfully navigate those potential future realities in ways that shape the future to address new ills and stressors on individuals, society, and the environment. Collectively, we want our actions to make for a far better world 10, 20, 30, 40, 50, and 100 years from now.

Thinking About Sustainable Development and Doughnut Economics

In studying and contemplating the chapters of this book, it is helpful for the reader to think in terms of two guiding meta concepts and their corresponding bodies of work. These are, namely, sustainable development and Doughnut Economics.

Sustainable development refers to the ongoing economic growth and prosperity of people groups around the world in ways that are sustainable in a number of key areas over the long term. These areas include economic, environmental, social, and political, amongst others.

The concept of sustainable development is best embodied in the United Nations *2030 Agenda for Sustainable Development*[2] (adopted by UN member states in September 2015), which espouses **17** integrated *Sustainable Development Goals* (*SDGs*) intended to end extreme poverty, reduce inequality, and protect the planet by 2030. The theme of this Agenda is "Leave No One Behind", and its 17 SDGs are the following:

1. No Poverty

2. Zero Hunger

3. Good Health and Well-Being

4. Quality Education

5. Gender Equality

6. Clean Water and Sanitation

7. Affordable and Clean Energy

8. Decent Work and Economic Growth

9. Industry, Innovation, and Infrastructure

10. Reduced Inequalities

11. Sustainable Cities and Communities

12. Responsible Consumption and Production

13. Climate Action

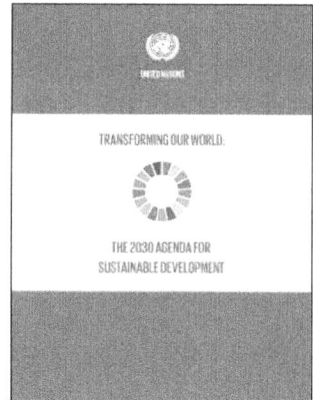

TRANSFORMING OUR WORLD:

THE 2030 AGENDA FOR
SUSTAINABLE DEVELOPMENT

14. Life Below Water

15. Life On Land

16. Peace, Justice, and Strong Institutions

17. Partnerships.

Doughnut Economics refers a simple, yet insightful and comprehensive model developed by Oxford Economist Kate Raworth in 2012, and later explained in her 2017 book Doughnut Economics: Seven Ways to Think Like a 21st Century Economist[3].

Doughnut Economics is itself a visual framework for sustainable development. It is shaped like a doughnut and combines the concept of social boundaries (its inner perimeter) with the complementary concept of ecological boundaries (its outer perimeter). It assesses the performance of a given economy according to the extent to which people's needs are met without overshooting Earth's ecological ceiling.

As shown in **Figure 1**, the model's inner perimeter consists of **12 social foundations**, these being: food security / health / education / income & work / peace & justice / political voice / social equity / gender equity / housing / networks / energy / water. Similarly, the model's outer perimeter consists of **9 ecological ceilings**, these being: climate change / ocean acidification / chemical pollution / nitrogen & phosphate loading / freshwater withdrawals / land conversion / biodiversity loss / air pollution / ozone layer depletion.

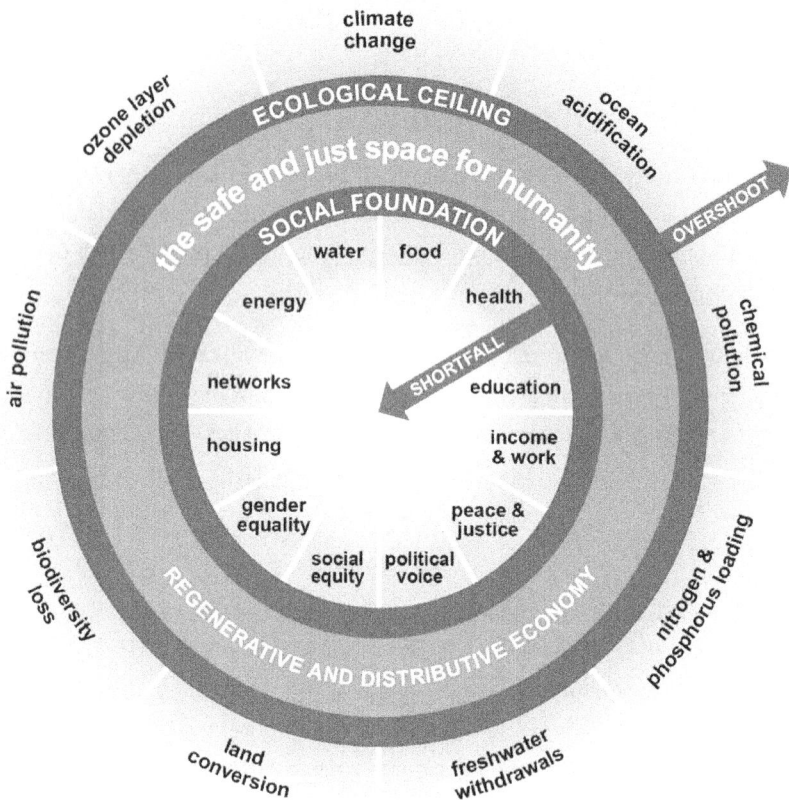

Figure 1: *The Doughnut Economics Model by Kate Raworth.*
Image courtesy of Wikimedia Commons.

The primary aim of this model is to help reframe developmental challenges and set sustainable goals for each one. According to the model, an economy is considered to be 'prosperous' when all twelve of its social foundations are met without overshooting any of its nine ecological ceilings, a condition represented by the area in between the model's inner and outer rings, and which, according to Raworth, is considered to be the safe and just space for humanity to operate within.

Back To Us

For the reader of this book, the challenges your business wrestles with may not impact these outcomes directly, but... they will impact them indirectly, and otherwise contribute to them, one way or the other.

This lies in such decisions as:

- the energy sources used to operate capital assets;
- the choice of materials used to produce material goods;
- the choice of production and distribution centers, and the corresponding amount of transportation involved in those activities;
- the deployment of new technologies and/or business models that enable new consumer behaviors.
- And so on.

And so the questions become ones of:

- Are these the most sustainable energy sources available to us?
- Are these the least impactful material choices available to us?
- Are these the least impactful production and distribution centers available to us?
- Will the new consumer behaviors we enable be positive or negative ones, and might there be secondary – perhaps unintended – behaviors with negative consequences, and if so, what safeguards can we incorporate to prevent or minimize such behaviors and consequences.
- And so on.

The choices that one's business makes in response to these and other questions will impact not only the business itself, and not only its customers and markets, but also society and the environment at large. Consequently, it is immensely important that each business consider and contemplate the answers to these questions in a holistic manner, taking into account the effects their decisions will have on societal, environmental, political, and economic systems around the world. This responsibility lies with each one of us.

Again, the purpose of this book is not to prescribe answers, but rather to evoke thoughtful questions. It is up to you, the reader, to weigh these questions carefully, and to come up with your own answers that will ensure we have all left the right legacy for our children and our children's children, and for all those who will come after them.

With that charge, press forward!

Anthony Mills
Executive Director
Global Innovation Institute
Autumn 2020

End Notes

1 The Limits to Growth: A Report for The Club of Rome's Project on the Predicament of Mankind, Donella H. Meadows, Dennis L. Meadows, Jørgen Randers, William W. Behrens III, Universe Books, 1972, https://clubofrome.org/publication/the-limits-to-growth/.

2 "Transforming Our World: The 2030 Agenda for Sustainable Development", A/RES/70/1, United Nations, New York, September 2015, https://sustainabledevelopment.un.org/post2015/transformingourworld/publication.

3 Doughnut Economics: Seven Ways to Think Like a 21st-Century Economist, Kate Raworth, Chelsea Green Publishing, February 2017, https://www.amazon.com/Doughnut-Economics-Seven-21st-Century-Economist/dp/1603587969.

CHAPTER 1

PURPOSE-DRIVEN INNOVATION

Dr. Larry Schmitt

Purpose-driven Innovation:
Achieving Balance in a Profit-driven World

Ever since Milton Friedman's 1970 NYT essay[1], governments, societies, and businesses have been arguing about the thesis that the sole responsibility of companies is to maximize owner profits.[2] This argument has grown louder, more nuanced, and more urgent over the past few years, and is now top-of-mind for some of the world's largest investors (BlackRock), most influential CEOs (Benioff), newest social movements (B-Corps), non-profits (JUST Capital), and influential government actors (Democratic Socialists). It is becoming increasingly clear that the imperative of purpose needs to be placed alongside that of profit as a motivating force in the future of business.

But what is purpose? Who gets to decide? Can purpose be measured? These are questions that can – and need – to be answered. We can start by looking at an example of an innovation, one that was devoid of any conception of social well-being or purpose, that went horribly wrong.

In 1987, bankers at Drexel Burnham Lambert (DBL)[3] created the first collateralized debt obligation, or CDO[4], a true innovation in the banking and finance industry. It would take 30 years for this innovation to contribute to one of the worst recessions in history. The CDO satisfied a market need and desire from two different customer segments – companies (and individuals) that needed debt funding but did not have good credit, and investors (mostly institutional) who wanted more fixed income investment alternatives[5].

DBL was known to be ruthlessly profit-driven and often challenged ethical and regulatory boundaries. It was, after all, the home of the infamous junk-bond king Michael Milken. DBL was forced into bankruptcy in 1990 but CDO's lived on. Despite its dubious practices, the banking innovators at DBL probably did not imagine that thirty years later their innovation would be the proximate cause of the worst global recession since the 1930s, but they probably could have – and should have. How did it all go so wrong?

As Max Wessel and Nicole Helmer state in their article "A Crisis of Ethics in Technology Innovation",[6]

> *If you're the executive who happens to decouple consumer protection from mortgage lending, all the positive intentions in the world won't protect you from the unavoidable backlash. Predicting where your industry will stumble within this new world can make the difference in ensuring your business flourishes with its reputation intact.*

Being a purpose-driven company is hard. Being a purpose-driven innovator within a purpose-driven company is hard. Being a purpose-driven innovator within a strictly profit-driven company is well-nigh impossible. But from the perspective of the innovator, there are things that can and should be done to move the needle on the purpose-driven dial.

A collective understanding of what tradeoffs (if any) need to be made between purpose and profits is becoming more holistic. We are starting to recognize the complexity of the business, governmental, and societal systems we operate in over longer time horizons. We are starting to recognize that the often-unintended negative effects of short-term thinking are now easily exposed, and the ramifications are greater. The threats to social well-being are rising and this creates forces that companies did not necessarily need to consider when Friedman's imperative was the predominant view.

While the threats to social well-being are rising, so are their visibility and the tools available to counter them. What is necessary is a world in which societal well-being is the vision and the driving force behind innovation, business creation, and profitable growth.

How will the multiple desires for societal well-being (and who gets to decide what this means) mesh with the capitalist imperatives of growth and profits?

How will the forces of society, government, and business interact with each other to achieve equilibrium that is stable? What will this equilibrium be in the future?

How can innovators, and the systems they build and use, deal with these tensions and have influence over the outcome?

The answer to these, and many other questions about purpose-driven innovation, is "it's complicated".

The Forces of Profit and Purpose

Virtue is excellence, something uncommonly great and beautiful, which rises far above what is vulgar and ordinary.

*Adam Smith – Author of **The Theory of Moral Sentiments**[7]*

Our collective understanding of what impacts investor returns is becoming more complex, more holistic, and more long-term. This shift is happening not because of altruism, but because of the realization that a long-term perspective actually can be more profitable. The implications of bad behavior are more easily exposed and the ramifications greater in the long run. The threats to humanity from terrorism, pandemics, climate change, economic insecurity, etc. are rising, and so are the unintended consequences of innovations that have global scope and power.

There is plenty of evidence that capitalism is a key creator of wealth and prosperity and will remain so for the foreseeable future. The world *will* remain a predominantly capitalistic world. The incentives are aligned for people to benefit from what capitalism creates and to accumulate wealth by working in, and investing in, profit-seeking corporations.

But capitalism is not guaranteed. Nor does it need to live within a democratic system (consider China with its combination of authoritarian government control and unfettered capitalism – including large doses of crony capitalism). Capitalism can also be corrupted. Examples of crony capitalism[8], corporate welfare[9], surveillance capitalism[10], abound. But capitalism does thrive in a democratic system where people can decide the relationship between business and government.

If laissez faire, capitalist approaches do not work to promote purpose-driven innovation, then, in democratic societies, the system can be changed. It is in the interest of businesses to ensure that future over-reaction does not result in onerous constraints imposed by policies and regulations. This means acting in the interest of society early on while there is still the freedom to do so, and, perhaps, accepting some self-imposed constraints up front instead of waiting for them to be imposed.

The question then is how to harness the forces of capitalism to do good rather than harm. Much has been written about this[11,12,13,14,15] and the consensus, supported by much evidence, is that capitalism and the profits it requires do not need to conflict with doing good. This is where the purpose-driven enterprise, and purpose-driven innovation, come in. Operating within a capitalistic framework, enterprises and individuals can create well-being while satisfying the profit objectives of those with capital.

Three Spheres of Influence and Control

Before discussing how an innovator can influence the purpose-driven motivations and objectives of an enterprise, we must discuss what it means to be a purpose-driven enterprise. There is a nebulous consensus that a purpose-driven enterprise should contribute to societal well-being. But what exactly is societal well-being and who gets to decide?

Three distinct spheres of power and influence that determine what is societal well-being are in constant flux and interaction.

- **Government**: Exerts influence and control though policies, practices, laws, and regulations. Positive influences (e.g., consumer protection, antitrust) can coexist with negative ones (e.g., corporate welfare, surveillance state).

- **Society**: Exerts influence and control through individual and collective reputation. This manifests as social pressure – both positive and negative. Because societies are comprised of individuals and communities, there can be many, often conflicting, pressures being expressed. Not all people agree on societal well-being.

- **Business**: Exerts influence and control through the artifacts that are brought into the world and the behaviors they exhibit with respect to their investors and stakeholders. Since one of the key stakeholders is the customer, customers' buying decisions have a powerful influence.

Individuals and groups act in all three spheres simultaneously and collectively achieve an equilibrium at any one point in time with the balance and tensions between the three spheres influencing each party's behavior. The behaviors (and balance) will be different in different nation-states and in different local and global communities and networks. The three spheres are sometimes in congruence, but many times they are in tension. At such times, a change in equilibrium can occur. It is those changes, which can be sudden and disruptive, that create both threats and opportunities.

In the long-term, it is societies and their governments that get to decide what is in the best interest of their constituent's long-term well-being. They do this through the mechanisms of reputation and regulation. But the process whereby a collective understanding of social good emerges, and the forces of reputation and regulation can exert their control, can be long and contentious. This dynamic is often characterized by 'punctuated equilibrium'[16] with long stretches of stasis, during which pressures build, and then periods of rapid change that are often unexpected but, in retrospect, become clear.

In this society-government-business trinity, it is the business enterprise which must make decisions that ultimately shape and influence how societies and governments will react. It is an enterprise's actions – through the introduction of innovations that change behaviors – that cause changes in reputation and regulation. An enterprise that seeks to understand these forces and the potential reactions of society and government will be well ahead of the game. An enterprise that seeks to make the societal and governmental reactions to its innovations positive or at least benign, is an enterprise that can rightfully be said to have a purpose-driven motivation.

Within the business sphere are distinct actors called enterprises. The term enterprise is used to encompass all types of value-creating entities and to highlight how companies, both young and old, can grow by being enterprising – devising new products, services, and ways to engage their employees. An enterprise is NOT a disembodied entity. It IS a collection of investors, leaders, and stakeholders.

Purpose-driven From an Enterprise Perspective

For an enterprise, purpose answers the question "How is the world a better place by your enterprise being here?"[17]   Making the world a 'better place' involves more than a company's good behavior. It also involves the long-term impact of the things they produce – and not just from a sustainability objective, but from an *effect on society* perspective. It is not enough to be sustainable and green or have a Corporate Social Responsibility (CSR) program, if your products themselves are causing harm.

There are two aspects to being purpose driven:

1. **Enterprise Behavior** – Is the enterprise a good citizen? How does it treat all its investors and stakeholders? What are the ways the company creates and gets its offerings into the world?

2. **Artifact Effects** – What are the effects, both intended and unintended, of the enterprise's products, services, and business models upon society? What happens when a company's offerings are adopted and used in both expected and unexpected ways?

Doing well at #1 does not necessarily mean doing well at #2. Facebook excels at #1. It treats its investors and stakeholders extremely well. Investors have reaped enormous returns (even though, with two classes of stock, most investors do not have any say in governance) and stakeholders have received enormous benefits. But at the start of the 2020s, there has been much evidence, and multiple voices from society and government saying, that Facebook is failing at #2. It is only when an enterprise is doing well at both that it can be called a truly purpose-driven enterprise.

Enterprise Behavior

There are many behaviors an enterprise can exhibit that benefit its investors and stakeholders. Virtually every large company, and many small ones as well, are adopting some version of purpose-driven under the banner of Corporate Social Responsibility (CSR), Enlightened Shareholder Value (ESV), Triple Bottom Line (PPP), Environmental, Social Governance (ESG), Sustainability, etc., designed to make the enterprise a 'good citizen'.

In his book <u>Grow the Pie</u>, author Alex Edmans[18] identifies the following categories of interested parties in a company's future well-being.

— **Investors** who are interested in **profits.**

— **Stakeholders** who are interested in various forms of **value**.

- **Colleagues** who are interested in their **livelihood**.

- **Customers** who are interested in the **surplus** an offering brings to them.

- **Suppliers** who are interested in the **funding** that comes from the success of the offering.

- **Environment** that is interested on **renewal** of its resources.

- **Government** that is interested in the **taxes** that support their services.

- **Communities** that are interested in the **vibrancy** that people and organizations bring.

A company that satisfies <u>all</u> these parties in the ways listed above results in what many would say is a purpose-driven enterprise. Yet, is this enough? Imagine a fictional firearms manufacturer (such as the formerly bankrupt Remington Arms Company) that follows all the tenets of triple-bottom-line, enlightened shareholder value, corporate social responsibility, sustainability, etc. They are doing everything that a purpose-driven advocate says you should do. But are they really purpose-driven? There is a sizable population in the U.S. that believes owning a gun (or guns) is a social good. A firearms company can also believe that it is a social good and have as its long-term mission 'A gun for every person'. But is this really what we mean by purpose-driven? What is missing in this equation?

Artifact Effects

What is missing are the long-term consequences of behaviors caused by an enterprise's innovative artifact being introduced into the world. The effects that the artifact has on society includes not just the product or service itself, but also the business model employed by the enterprise to get these artifacts into customers' hands and to influence how customers use them. Without consideration of these effects, all the triple-bottom-line efforts in the world can be for naught.

To imagine all the effects an innovation could have on society, an enterprise must broaden its scope beyond just their direct customer's perspective. Their perspective must include the secondary and tertiary effects of their direct customer's behaviors. These are the 'externalities' that are not often considered, but they are the externalities to which societies and governments will eventually pay attention. These externalities need to be brought 'inside' and made visible if a company is to have hope of being purpose driven.

Consider our hypothetical firearms manufacturer. If they were to do this – that is, consider the long-term secondary and tertiary effects of their offerings – one option[19] would be to reimagine their offerings and business model to:

- Incorporate smart-gun technology.
- Support fingerprint technology meant to prevent anyone who is not the gun's owner from firing it.
- Add an identity stamp to ammunition fired from any of its guns.
- Establish and standardize responsible sales policies for retailers to sell its firearms.
- Lobby for reasonable gun control legislation.

These new innovations (all of which have long been proposed in one form or another), along with others that have not yet been imagined, would be driven by the purpose-driven future of a society in which gun ownership is a social good. The problem is that when even some of these have been tried, the backlash from current customers and social actors has been intense. So much so that it would take a company with a true purpose-driven vision to stand up to the short-term pressure from those who want the status-quo.

Another example of an unexpected reaction to a purpose-driven innovation is the case of Golden Rice[20], an innovation that uses the technology of gene editing to induce normal rice to produce beta-carotene. Golden Rice is a genetically-modified organism (GMO) that is designed to address childhood death and blindness, primarily in Asia and Africa, due to lack of vitamin A. This is a condition that is estimated to kill 670,000 children under the age of 5 and cause an additional 500,000 cases of irreversible childhood blindness **each year**. Surely this would be an unmitigated benefit for society and the communities that suffer from vitamin A deficiency.

Surprisingly, the perspective that this is a societal good is not universally shared. Aside from the technical and development issues of getting a commercially viable and effective Golden Rice (something that was done by 2005), it is still not widely grown and used where it is most needed. There has been a sustained and unrelenting effort on the part of anti-GMO groups (and others) to block its use.

In the meantime, despite alternative methods of providing vitamin A to poor populations, many millions of children have needlessly died or gone blind over the 15 years since golden rice has been ready for the world to use. Is Golden Rice a social good? Did the anti-GMO people think they were promoting a social good? Could any of this have been anticipated and counteracted?

Who is the Judge of Social Well-being?

As mentioned above, the ultimate arbiters of social good are societies and governments, either through their action or inaction. But the judgment of these diffuse bodies often comes late and is not always perfectly clear. In the interim, it is the enterprise itself, and especially its board and executives (in concert with their investors) who must make the decisions about how the company behaves and what new innovations to introduce into the world. And boards and executives are notoriously wary of being the judges of what is right and wrong. They really do not want to be the arbiters of social good because, by doing so, they will invariably make some people angry.

But willful ignorance is no solution. It is much better to have *a-priori* knowledge, ideas, and plans rather than be forced into a *post-hoc* reaction. But *post-hoc* reaction seems to be the norm. In a June 2020 NYT Op-ed[21], Kara Swisher comments on the actions of a new tech startup called Robinhood and an incident in which one of its users committed suicide because he mistakenly thought that he had accumulated $730,000 in debt. In her Op-ed, Ms. Swisher writes:

> [A big question] has been plaguing the tech industry and its innovative entrepreneurs for far too long: What is the reason for their persistent tendency to ignore the potentially dangerous impacts of their creations? These days the companies can seem not just careless but also predatory.

Is it to make more money? Is it because growth trumps safety? Is it rank sloppiness? Lack of foresight? A design flaw that could have and, more to the point, should have been anticipated? A laser focus on innovation? Or all of the above?

Perhaps the reason hardly matters, since, as Robert Louis Stevenson wrote, "Everyone, at some time or another, sits down to a banquet of consequences."

This is a damning indictment of the fact that we still do not have good ways to figure out the future personal and societal effects of our innovations. Yet the visibility of effects is increasing dramatically. Without social media, this story would never have become known. There are several billion people watching and commenting on the actions of companies and the effects of their products. Each one of them with their own opinion about what is good and what is not.

The fact is that different people and communities, both outside the company and within, will have different – sometimes diametrically opposed – ideas on what is socially beneficial. The innovator needs to have a strong voice in this conversation. How can this be done?

Another Innovator's Dilemma

A recurrent theme here is that decisions, small decisions, that look perfectly fine at the time you make them can still lead to outcomes that are quite a bit different than how you imagined them. The larger effect is that you can make perfectly good decisions and still end up at a place that you can conclude that this is not the right outcome in some general sense of what right outcomes should be.

Sridhar Ramaswamy – Former Head of Google Ads

Clayton Christensen published his seminal work The Innovator's Dilemma in 1997.[22] Since then, the research and practice of innovation has expanded to encompass all aspects of the science and practice of innovation. But even though Christensen was very much interested in the subject of 'purpose-driven' in some of his other work[23], over the past 20+ years, this aspect of innovation has been very lightly addressed by innovation researchers and practitioners.

It is easy to see why this is so. After all, included in virtually every definition of innovation is the concept of creating value, both for the customer and for the company. Something is not considered to be an innovation unless it is valued by customers enough to cause them to adopt the new thing, and to also create economic value for the company providing that thing. If a customer wants something, then, in some sense, it must be 'good'.

This perspective, though helpful, ignores two aspects that a purpose-driven view of innovation must consider. The first aspect is that in many cases, the 'innovator' is a company and the customer is also a company (business-to-business – B2B). This immediately raises the question of how a company's motivations are translated into their customer company's motivations. Even if a company is purpose-driven, if their company customers are not, then the definition of 'good' becomes muddled by what the company's customers do with the innovation. Even if the customer is an individual, what assurances are there that that individual has the same perception of social well-being as the company?

The second aspect, one that is often ignored, is that nearly all the study and practice of innovation focuses on the time period from first conception to launch (and sometimes scale). At some point around the launch of an innovation, the operational mind and muscles of a company take over. The long-term impact of an innovation is usually only discussed in terms of revenue and profit growth projections as well as issues of warranty and liability for certain products. The impact is not considered in terms of long-term societal well-being except in retrospect, often after something has gone very wrong.

The fact is that virtually all innovators want to have positive impact on the world. But innovators often give up their influence too early and too easily. Others take over and when they do, they are often in a poor position to see all the possible consequences the innovation may have. History is rife with examples of an innovator's good intentions gone awry. Why does this happen? What are the forces that cause this to happen and how could these forces, and their unexpected outcomes, be made visible?

There are two factors at work that push against the purpose-driven innovator and get in the way, no matter how much an innovator – be they an individual, team, or company – wishes to benefit society.

1. **Loss of control** and influence – internally & externally.

2. Blindness to long-term **future consequences** – both good and bad.

It is impossible to be a purpose-driven innovator within a company that is not purpose-driven. But within a purpose-driven company, given the two factors above, it can still be difficult for an innovator to advance the purpose-driven motivations of the company they are part of. What are the ways an innovator can have influence over the trajectory of their innovation as it moves from idea to its manifestation in the world – in multiple instances and multiple forms?

Loss of Control

We also had really long and important and tortured discussions for example around should Google data ever be used for serving ads off of Google. This went through an incredible amount of debate. But there is always competitive pressure. Facebook was doing this already. That plays into the calculus that goes on.

Sridhar Ramaswamy – Former Head of Google Ads

There are two compelling forces that overtake the good intentions of an innovator and result in the innovator's loss of control.

1. Within a company, as an innovation is launched and scaled, the locus of influence and decision-making moves away from the innovation team to a broader coalition of decision makers. Company imperatives of growth and profit drive the need to create organizational infrastructure to support the business built around the innovation. Internal control transfers from inventor to innovator to entrepreneur to manager to executive.

2. External forces of adoption and adaptation create trajectories for the innovation that are unexpected. External influence, both intentional and unintentional, broadens from the company to their customers to their ecosystem and to society.

The effect of this is that the locus of making sure the innovation is creating both economic value and social good – the ostensible motivations of a purpose-driven company – becomes widely dispersed and no longer resides solely within the innovator's or the company's direct control or influence.

Even within a company, innovators lose control over how their innovation will be scaled. This inevitably occurs in organizations large and small when an innovation is taken over by an existing business or the company puts a business executive in charge of scaling. If the company still answers to the Friedman doctrine, the innovation will inevitably be co-opted to generate the maximum possible near-term revenue and profits.

In addition to internal loss of control, innovators, and the companies they are a part of, lose even more control once the innovation is out in the world. Other things happen that are not only beyond the innovator's control but are beyond the company's control as well. These can have future consequences that are unintended and unexpected. The unintended consequences of globally adopted social media used for disinformation influence, facial recognition that is used for surveillance, and ever-present AI used to predict the behavior with everyone with a cellphone, are just a few examples that, as of 2020, were playing out in real time.

How can an innovator, and the innovation systems they build, mitigate unanticipated and negative outcomes? How can innovators balance the profit-driven and the purpose-driven motivations that are needed in today's world? How can innovators have more influence on how corporations ensure that their innovations do not result in negative outcomes? Should this even be a concern to the innovation profession, or should it be left to the corporate stakeholders to decide?

The answers to these questions, and many others, are at the forefront of what the next era of purpose-driven innovation will look like. New innovation methods and tools that did not exist even ten years ago are now available to potentially address these questions. And new innovation methods and tools are constantly being created to deal with the increasingly volatile and complex world. Innovators are up to the task. They just need to have the influence they deserve.

But influence can be hard to come by. Innovators are not the ones who have final control over how their innovations are used, no matter what their intentions. It is the corporate leaders, investors, governments, and societies who determine how something new to the world will be used.

Future Consequences

Unintended consequences get to the heart of why you never really understand an adaptive problem until you have solved it. Problems morph and 'solutions' often point to deeper problems. In social life, as in nature, we are walking on a trampoline. Every inroad reconfigures the environment we tread on.

Richard Pascale – Author of _The Power of Positive Deviance_[24]

Innovations, especially the most transformational ones, inevitably have long-term, unexpected, and unintended consequences. But innovators and business leaders alike typically obsess over the immediate future where the impact of even the most transformational innovation is often quite muted. Consider Facebook when it introduced its mobile and advertising platforms. In the first couple of years, the effects were interesting but hardly the society-changing ones that would eventually emerge.

It is the long-term future consequences that are often the most significant and the hardest to imagine upfront. It should be within the innovator's charter to try.

In economic terms, knowledge and ideas are non-rivalrous and non-excludable. They are undiminished by 'consumption' and it is not possible to restrict others from using them. At most, they can be temporarily hidden or protected via government mechanisms such as patents and copyrights, but even these can often be circumvented. Any innovation can be corrupted. This is ultimately the root cause of both loss of control and unexpected future consequences.

The trajectory of an innovation is determined by many forces that are beyond the direct control of the organization that introduces it. They are what can 'mess up' the good intentions of an innovator. Take the case of Drexel Burnham Lambert and their invention of the Collateralized Debt Obligation (CDO) mentioned previously. What happened after they were released into to the world?

— The company **evolved** CDOs into other forms and uses – DBL itself took the concept and applied it to many different types of asset loans and risk profiles. They created an algorithmic calculation of risk and promoted it to customers seeking new investment options.

- Customers put them to **alternative uses** – the customers of CDOs saw the potential and demanded more of what they wanted (i.e., risk defined returns). In addition, other 'non-customers', such as insurance companies like AIG, created their own insurance innovations to support the CDO ecosystem. This was the direct cause of AIG needing to be bailed out by the government during the Great Recession in 2008.

- Competitors **appropriated** the concept – once DBL created the CDO, it was clear to others that they could too. The CDO concept is a non-rival, non-exhaustible good. It can be copied and mutated at will. This is what happened. Others, equally uninterested in the potential consequences, saw what a CDO could do for their business and copied it to suit their own purposes.

- Societies and governments only slowly created **reputation and policy** in response to the effects of the CDO. Society was slow to assign responsibility and to allocate blame and the poor reputation of the CDO emerged only after its destructive effects were felt. The US Federal Reserve, the US Securities and Exchange Commission (SEC), and the entire financial oversight ecosystem were slow to realize what was happening and slow to respond.

Different communities have different explanations of what went wrong. Some financial analysts see the cause of the recession being individuals who took out loans they couldn't possibly afford. Others see the cause being the predatory practices of enterprises pushing offerings onto customers that could not understand the consequences. Years later, consensus on the cause is still being debated. The result is universally condemned.

The question that a purpose-driven innovator should be asking is not then who decides, but rather what are all the possible and plausible consequences that can be foreseen when one considers the primary, secondary, and tertiary implications of their innovation. Once some of the plausible consequences are described – the good and bad – then it is possible to provide a degree of transparency of possible outcomes. This lets all the actors who will be affected in the long term to contribute to the judgement of future social impact.

A solution is needed that can help companies work through the anxiety of being arbiters of social good. It needs to be a solution that makes long-term consequences visible and allow all types of actors in all three spheres of influence to weigh in.

An Innovator's Solution

Without reflection, we go blindly on our way, creating more unintended consequences, and failing to achieve anything useful.

Margaret Wheatley – Author of <u>Leadership and the New Science</u>[25]

Today, purpose-driven outcomes are achieved through idiosyncratic and ad-hoc means. The future will see this process become more systematized. New methods and tools, ones that do not exist today, will be required. This systemization of purpose-driven processes is just beginning.

For an innovation to be purpose-driven, two things are necessary:

- The <u>company</u> must be purpose-driven and trust that this will maximize its long-term profits.

- In addition to the business-driven issues that are always considered, the internal and external <u>purpose-driven issues</u> inherent in any new innovation must be revealed and acted upon.

But because, in a large organization, the innovator does not have ultimate control, it is unclear how purpose-driven innovators, even with prescient foresight of how their innovation could be used for good (or for bad), can have influence. These are the two issues that need to be dealt with.

1. How should purpose-driven innovators expand the scope of their <u>insights</u> to see all the implications of their innovation?

2. How can purpose-driven innovators have <u>influence</u> over the entities that will ultimately control how the new innovation will exist in the world?

Answering these two questions is key to whether purpose-driven innovation can be a real thing.

Expanding Scope

Since <u>The Innovator's Dilemma</u>[26] was published in 1997, the corporate innovator's and the innovation world's attention has been on the new artifact – the new product or service, the new business model, etc. And their focus has been on methods such as *Voice-of-the-Customer* and *Jobs-to-be-Done*[27]. Entire innovation practices have sprung into being to teach and support open innovation, design thinking, customer journeys, agile development, minimal viable product, and test and learn. Tools such as the Business Model Canvas[28, 29] and idea management systems have become ubiquitous.

What these have in common is the implicit constraint on the timeframe of their applicability and the scope of their effects. Although long-term futures may be considered during creative exercises, the focus of attention is squarely on the innovation as it moves from idea to launch and scale. This means that the immediate future, what happens right after launch, is front and center. Long-term considerations are relegated to the background.

In addition, the scope of impact considered is generally constrained to immediate customers, suppliers, channels, etc., and perhaps their direct connections. Rarely are the secondary and tertiary effects considered.

In a world of purpose-driven innovation, this is not enough. Because of unintended consequences and significant externalities, a purpose-driven innovator can no longer be oblivious to, and claim ignorance about, how their innovation will affect the wider world in the longer term. If a purpose-driven innovator truly seeks to have impact and change the world, they cannot shirk the obligation to foresee a complete picture of how the world can plausibly change – for the good and for the bad.

Exerting Influence

An innovator's loss of control is inevitable. Once an innovation starts to become real, even as early as the creation of a minimal viable product, it will require resources that do not necessarily come from the innovator or innovation team. It will receive management attention and become part of a portfolio. When it gets to the incubation stage, others within and outside the company will have a say in how the innovation is designed and built. This loss of control is inevitable, but it is also necessary. Others are going to take an innovation in unexpected – and sometimes detrimental – directions.

While an innovator cannot avoid the inevitable loss of control, they can and should retain influence well beyond the traditional role they are relegated to. The effectiveness of an innovator to have on-going influence over how their innovation evolves can be one of the most powerful forces that supports the purpose-driven objectives of an enterprise.

The way that innovators can and must retain ongoing influence is to make visible – to colleagues, business executives, society, and government policymakers and regulators – the plausible future consequences of something that is new to the world. This means the positive and the negative, the intended and the unintended consequences.

Within a company, where an innovator has initial control and (hopefully) significant influence, one possible method for influence can be found in an extension of the Business Model Canvas. This can be called the **Social Model Canvas**. Like a business model, the social model defines the rules of the game that is being played – what is allowable and what is not. In a business model, these rules relate to commerce – the ways the company's customers and partners exchange value and are engaged by the company. In a social model, they relate to something much bigger and longer-term.

The Social Model Canvas –
A Tool for the Purpose-driven Innovator

If innovators are to have an influence with purpose-driven outcomes, they need <u>tools</u> to lead a company in their purpose-driven strategy. Among the methods and tools to help do this is an expansion of the *Business* Model Canvas[30] to turn it into a *Social* Model Canvas.

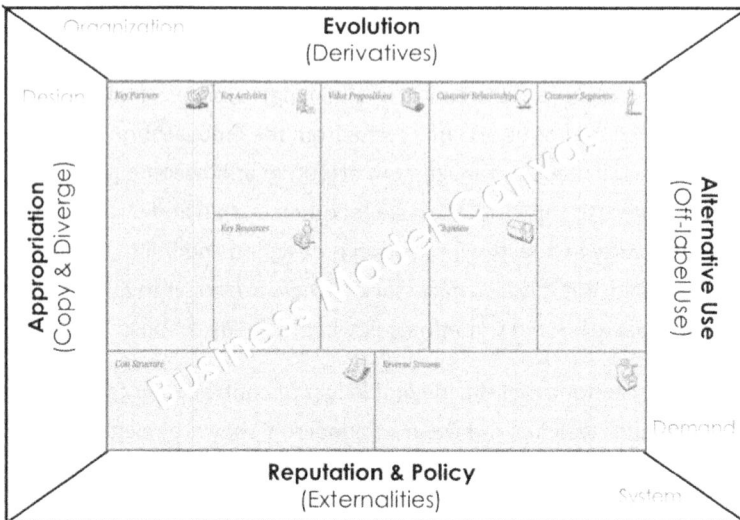

Figure 2: *The Social Model Canvas.*

The Social Model Canvas is constructed as an enhancement of the Business Model Canvas with an additional layer that expands the canvas to illuminate the primary, secondary, and tertiary effects of an innovation along four distinct dimensions. It is designed to promote the imagining of <u>alternate futures</u>, both good and bad. It broadens the context for the innovation being considered and extends the timeframe beyond what is normally considered.

By using the Social Model Canvas, an innovator can make potential future consequences, both good and bad, visible to all parties, inside and outside the company, who have a stake in the long-term outcomes. Doing this can help a company abide by their purpose-driven mission.

The Social Model Canvas does all this by guiding the innovator to consider each of the following four areas of investigation.

Evolution (Organization)

After an innovation is introduced into the world, its <u>evolution</u> involves all the subsequent updates, modifications, releases, and derivative offerings a company creates to expand its initial scope. This results in multiple, branching trajectories that, over time, create a highly branched, dense tree of products, services, and business models. This branched tree of future trajectories can be thoughtfully anticipated, not by figuring out <u>all</u> future paths and possibilities that might be predicted, but by looking ahead at <u>plausible trajectories</u>. In this way, an innovator can not only gain insight into future business possibilities, they can also see places where the societal well-being outcomes could possibly go awry.

Examining the long-term evolution driven by the organization can help illuminate how the company can and should move the innovation forward to advance both its economic and social benefit objectives.

Alternative Use (Demand)

Companies are almost always surprised at the unexpected uses their innovations are put to by their customers, and often do not consider the entire lifecycle of their innovation after it gets into their customers' hands. There is an entire segment of innovation study that focuses on alternative use as a source of new ideas[31]. Instead of waiting, observing, and being surprised, the innovator can and should anticipate alternative uses and the entire lifecycle of their innovation – and how the company should and could influence these.

What are the unexpected ways that not just current customers, but future customers, will use the thing that is being introduced? How will the company deal with 'off-label' use? What will the company do if customers start using the new thing in ways that are counter to the company's purpose-driven mission? How does the innovation 'age', and eventually get replaced? What should the company encourage or discourage?

Appropriation (Design)

It is inevitable that, no matter your IP position, others will appropriate, to one degree or another, any new innovation introduced into the market. An example of this is Facebook copying Snapchat's 'Stories' feature[32]. This appropriation will be done by other enterprises that do not necessarily have the same purpose-driven motivations or ideas about social well-being as the company that introduces the innovation. It is up to the innovator to think about how others will appropriate the new concepts and use them to their own ends and how the company can control or influence how the concept and its underlying technology is used.

How will others appropriate the concepts and use them to their own ends? How will you deal with copying and redesigning by others? What are the design boundaries – how could the innovation be shaped and altered to do something different? Can the company control or influence how the concept and its underlying technology is used?

Reputation & Policy (System)

The triple forces of evolution, alternative use, and appropriation create responses from societies and governments. These reinforcing and balancing feedforward and feedback loops determine future reputation (from Society) and policy (from Government). This is a complex, dynamic system that is often difficult to understand in the present, much less in the future.

These dynamics are often considered to be externalities by an enterprise that takes the position "we'll deal with the consequences when they happen". But this is not what a purpose-driven enterprise or a purpose-driven innovator should do.

The unintended effects of an innovation will eventually be responded to through social reputation and government policy and regulation. This creates an imperative for an innovator to be a social and policy futurist and advocate. This may require the innovator, and their company, to go against the natural, immediate instinct of the company at times and to advocate for things that may impact maximum growth and profits in the short term but which will ultimately result in a better, long-term outcome for society.

What are the appropriate externalities to consider and how should the company prepare to deal with them? What can the enterprise control, partially control, and have limited influence over? What are the levers of a company's influence?

Using the Social Model Canvas to Realize Purpose and Profit

It is often difficult to imagine a different world. It is this failure of imagination that so often leads to strategic surprise. What is needed is to expand the futures that are considered by sparking the imagination.

Rita McGrath – Author of _Seeing Around Corners_[33]

Using the social-model canvas will expand futures that are considered. The four segments are used to open up the imagination and promote narratives that illuminate positive and negative consequences that could happen years from now. They are intended to get the innovator to think about implications beyond just success as measured by immediate growth and customer excitement. They are meant to counter the rosy scenarios that almost always accompany the launch of something new and to think about the potential downsides and unintended outcomes that accompany innovations that change human behavior.

In working through the Social Model Canvas, here are a few questions an innovator should address:

1. What are alternative futures besides the preferred one (the one that internal company projections are based on)?

2. What are secondary and tertiary effects of the innovation on both customers and non-customers?

3. What is considered to be outside the company's boundaries (externalities)? What would the company do if these were no longer externalities but something the company could control?

4. How do the four dimensions of Evolution, Alternative Use, Appropriation, and Reputation & Policy intersect with each other to create second- and third-order consequences?

5. To whom should the company communicate or warn about plausible downsides?

As an example, consider what happened with facial recognition in 2020. For years, the technology of facial recognition had been improving. Huge amounts had been invested in its technology and application. It had gotten to the point where a good facial recognition system can recognize someone at virtually any age in any pose. The benefits were many – from automatically tagging people in your photo album to providing privacy and security for everything you do with your smartphone.

But the downsides of facial recognition have also since been made visible. Facial recognition has made the surveillance society more likely[34]. Companies with questionable intent have appropriated the technology to do things that others find troubling.[35] Consequently, some companies have even gone so far as to voluntarily abandon or pause their facial recognition efforts and have asked governments to intervene.[36, 37] This is what imagination of alternative futures and visibility across all potential actors can and should do. It should have, and could have, been done much sooner.

To move into the realm of purpose-driven innovation, an innovator, and the company they are part of, must do the following.

– Expand the timeframe beyond what is normally considered.

– Look beyond direct effects to imagine secondary and tertiary effects of the innovation.

– Incorporate the methods and tools of the futurist and the strategist into the process.

– Acknowledge both the good and the bad outcomes and be clear about each.

– Become an advocate of transparency within and outside the company.

– Be a thought leader of the purpose-driven mission of the company.

The Social Model Canvas (among other methods and tools) can help the innovator accomplish these things, but most of all it will take a change in mindset on the part of the innovator and the company to realize that their social responsibility extends <u>far beyond</u> the products and services they build.

The Purpose of the Purpose-driven Innovator

The payoff of delaying gratification or making long-term choices is becoming greater and greater because of the institutions, society and culture we've set up. And yet our paleolithic minds seem to be wired to prioritize the immediate outcome.

James Clear – Author of <u>Atomic Habits</u>,[38]
as quoted in Creatures of Habit[39]

Enterprises need to go beyond initiatives like Corporate Social Responsibility (CSR), Enlightened Shareholder Value (ESV), Environmental Social Governance (ESG), triple bottom line, sustainability, and other movements that focus on corporate behavior but don't take into account long-term effects of the artifacts they introduce into the world. Friedman used economic value as a lowest common denominator because he thought individuals should make their own choices on deploying wealth for economic good. But that was too low a standard. The issue is that *economic value* is only a small part of the total value an enterprise creates for its investors. This is itself only a small part of the total consequences enterprises create in society through both their actions and the artifacts they introduce into the world.

Not every innovation goes as spectacularly wrong as Collateralized Debt Obligations did. But every innovation, even the most seemingly benign, has within it the seeds of both social good and social harm, and the forces of social pressure and government regulation will eventually intervene. But the mechanism of intervention may not be what is desired by an enterprise. It may seem for a while that the negative effects of an innovation are being ignored by society, that everything is going well – until it doesn't. This behavior of punctuated equilibrium – nothing seems to happen for a long time and then sudden and large change – is a challenge for all enterprises.

The new challenge for innovators is to foresee these sudden changes, what Rita McGrath calls *inflection points*, so that enterprise decisions and actions can happen in the seemingly 'quiet' period and eliminate, or at least mitigate, future negative consequences.

The world is rife with examples of significant innovations gone both right and wrong – in multiple ways. The examples used here – Collateralized Debt Obligations, Firearms, Golden Rice, Facial Recognition – are joined by virtually every other significant innovation ever created. There has probably never been a significant innovation for which the *a priori* question of whether it will be good or bad for society would not have had people arguing on both sides.

Purpose-driven Innovation and Capitalism

Like it or not, capitalism will remain alive and well. In a capitalist world, economic value will continue to be one of the major metrics of success. But economic value can be deployed in ways that either promote or that counter both individual and society *values*.

Capitalism is the most effective way of creating new value, of satisfying ever evolving and expanding individual and collective wants. But capitalism does not mean unfettered or even laissez faire behavior. It does not mean Friedman's vision of profit as a company's sole reason for being. Capitalism can live with purpose. The two are not incompatible. Being a purpose-driven enterprise may even be a way to propel the good outcomes of capitalism to a new level.

The concept of the corporation, or in more general terms an enterprise, is changing. We often assume that the current forms of capitalism and the corporation have been around forever, but they are actually relatively modern concepts and have been evolving, often rapidly, since their inception. We are in a new era of evolution in which the new shape of capitalism and corporations will take on decidedly purpose-driven forms. It is up to the purpose-driven innovator to help this to happen.

Motivations and Incentives

Purpose-driven means not having to squeeze through the narrow-waist of economic returns to get to the expression of people's different values. A new, purpose-driven innovation system must, of necessity, concern itself with the whole picture. One test of a well-designed purpose-driven framework would be that it supports different enterprises in different social and government systems because they have different conceptions of social well-being. This will allow enterprises to express their purpose in ways that suits the creation of economic value.

What really needs to change in the practice of innovation? What incentives need to be put in place for the practice of purpose-driven innovation to become standard? Unless there are either incentives or restrictions (regulation), it won't happen. Individual self-motivation will not be enough.

It is not enough for innovators to only focus on the good their innovation can do. But it is also not solely within their power to control how a new artifact will (or should be) used. Once an innovation is released into the world, the forces of influence and control expand exponentially and it is no longer possible for an individual, a team, or even a company, to control what happens. But they can still have influence.

Innovators need to be in a position to articulate policy-influencing concepts that promote changes in the government, society, and business systems that are in place. Instead of being powerless to swim upstream against the system, they can be the oracles of the future who indicate that a system must change before, instead of after, the bad stuff happens. The forces and voices for making enterprises more purpose-driven, and more long-term are emerging and they are becoming louder and more influential.[40, 41, 42] But there are also those who are pushing back.[43] In order for the forces of change to prevail, it will take not just a new generation of innovators, it will take changes to the system itself.

Innovators Must be Futurists and Strategists

An enterprise needs to address their purpose-driven vision at the level of long-term corporate strategy. They need investors and stakeholders who believe in the strategy. They need the systems, processes, and tools to implement that strategy. And they need the relationships – with their business ecosystem, society, and governments – to ensure that they are not disadvantaged by their purpose-driven strategy. Without a purpose-driven strategy, purpose-driven innovation will fail. In addition, to achieve a purpose-driven strategy, purpose-driven innovation is a necessity.

For this reason, innovators need to adopt many of the practices, mindsets, and tools of the futurist and the strategist. They need to go beyond the value proposition, the jobs-to-be-done, and the business model canvas. They need to make the future trajectories of their innovations – both good and bad – visible and actionable.

The Innovator as Futurist

To think like a futurist an innovator must be able to imagine the future as it could plausibly be. In one sense, innovators already do this. They imagine a future in which their innovation exists and how the intended customer will experience the new thing. The problem is that this view is often very limited and constrained to the specific customer and what is immediately affected by intended use. The tools of the futurist are much more expansive. They take into account not just the immediate customer, but also the entire complex ecosystem within which the new thing exists. Not only does the innovation affect the customer's experience, it causes changes in behaviors that ripple far and wide, with secondary and tertiary effects.

The methods of the futurist require imagination, systems thinking, world-building, and the ability to see the world as it could exist at both the high-level and the detailed level at the same time. It requires the ability to hold multiple perspectives in mind at the same time... to keep the whole and the parts in mind at once... the ability to go from the specific to the general and back again at will... the ability to connect levels and see the forest and the trees at once. It requires the innovator and the strategist to connect the levels and easily move between high, low, and mid-levels of abstraction. It demands that one not get stuck in the weeds or in the clouds and understand that insights at one level inform understanding at higher and lower levels. In addition, it requires that the innovator-futurist keep conflicting and opposing information in mind at once and use this tension to foster creativity.

The Innovator as Strategist

To think like a strategist an innovator must be able to create innovations that contribute to the long-term strategic purpose of the organization. The tools of the strategist are many and varied. From SWOT analysis to Porter's 5 Forces to scenario analysis, many of the strategy tools complement and overlap with the types of methods and tools that innovators are familiar with.

What the strategist can bring to the innovator is a broad perspective and context. The strategist's world is not just about a specific innovation, it is about the business and company as a whole and how it exists in its continually evolving ecosystem. The best strategists are systems thinkers. They recognize the interconnectedness and complexity of the overarching system that includes business, government, and society as co-equal influencers, and they take into account all these factors.

Unfortunately, the strategist's methods and tools are most often applied in service of the yearly strategic planning ritual. This is typically focused on the near-term (1-2 year time horizon) and makes extensive use of business intelligence (mostly of competitors), data collection, and analytic prediction.

What purpose-driven innovation can bring to strategy is a longer-term perspective. In addition to the near-term focused strategic plan, the foresight methods and tools of innovation can be used to create a dual path strategy[44] that takes into account the longer-term future where data-driven, predictive analytics are no longer useful. The Social Model Canvas is one of these tools that starts where near-term, strategic scenario analysis leaves off.

The intersection of strategy and innovation is inevitable (and necessary). Unless you have a strategy that has innovation at its core – unless you have an innovation system that is driven by strategy – you will not thrive in a purpose-driven world. Innovation needs to have influence at the level of business strategy or it will be ineffective at anything other than generating profits.

Being a Purpose-driven Innovator – It's Complicated

Being a purpose-driven innovator is <u>not</u> an easy task. Not only will the purpose-driven innovator need to deal with the myriad issues required to take an idea from concept to reality, they will now be asked to go further and imagine what a new reality could be like and prepare both the company and society for the consequences.

The rapidly changing world is making this more possible and more difficult at the same time.

- Technology (e.g., new/social media, etc.) will bring new degrees of transparency as well as greater influence of individuals (stakeholders and others). The tools of influence and advocacy are getting increasingly powerful, both for the innovator and for their supporters and adversaries. A company cannot be only about profit because people aren't only about profit. People themselves are purpose-driven.

- But people don't all have a shared purpose. The challenge of being purpose-driven will *always* be a mix of success and failure from any specific outside perspective. Every action a firm might take (intentional and unintentional) will have both good and bad in it.

- Companies must spot these potential successes and failures in advance by considering their intended aims, as well as any unintended consequences (first and second order) and how different ecosystem participants will perceive them. The Social Model Canvas is one tool that can help with this.

- Companies will need to be intentional about closing the loop for better feedback and influence by incorporating more (1) transparency, (2) sentiment sensing, (3) implication tracking, and (4) changes to their own intentions.

Capitalism will remain the predominant driver of wealth creation for the foreseeable future. Within the capitalist system, purpose-driven enterprises will eventually become predominant because they will generate better long-term value. Within the purpose-driven enterprise, innovators will have the opportunity to become key arbiters of purpose – being willing and able to foresee the future consequences of the things they bring into the world and thereby retaining influence over what happens to them and to society.

Becoming a purpose-driven innovator will become one of the most important roles within the enterprise, no matter what level within the organization someone is. It is inevitable.

Key Takeaways

Every innovator has, as one of their motivations, the desire to have positive impact in the world. But, in addition to the positive effects that innovations have on their customers and society, they often have unexpected and unintended consequences. This includes being co-opted by their own company, their customers, or their competitors who adhere to the Friedman doctrine that the only responsibility companies have is to maximize shareholder profits.[45]

The choices of companies, the innovations they pursue, and the effects on society are all connected. As innovators, our imperative is to influence the balance between profits and a deeper purpose that's needed in today's world.

- Businesses operate in a complex environment where the forces of investors, stakeholders, society, and government interact in unexpected and unanticipated ways, producing both positive and negative outcomes which are hard to anticipate.

- A purpose-driven enterprise works to mitigate the negative consequences of both their behavior and business model, and the products and services their customers use. But a company cannot control all the effects that their innovations may cause.

- One of the key jobs of a purpose-driven innovator is to anticipate and communicate the potential, long-term consequences of their work. A tool to help with this is the Social Model Canvas. This provides business, society, and government a means to engage earlier so as to influence how their innovations impact society.

- Promoting purpose-driven innovation in a capitalist system, with numerous different societies and governments that look at social well-being in different ways, is difficult but possible. In fact, it's becoming an imperative for the innovation profession.

End Notes

1 "Maximizing Profits: Milton Friedman", Open Textbooks for Hong Kong, 15 January 2016, http://www.opentextbooks.org.hk/ditatopic/19974.

2 An often-overlooked aspect of Friedman's perspective is that he believed in social well-being, he just thought that it was best served by returning profits to the investors who could then use the profits as they saw fit.

3 Wikipedia entry on *Drexel Burnham Lambert*, https://en.wikipedia.org/wiki/Drexel_Burnham_Lambert.

4 "Collateralized Debt Obligations and the Credit Crisis", Paul Conley, *The Balance*, 14 October 2019, https://www.thebalance.com/cdos-credit-crisis-417122.

5 Numerous deep and detailed analyses of CDOs have been written. "On the Mechanism of CDOs behind the Current Financial Crisis…" is just one of them – https://file.scirp.org/pdf/IIM20100200010_40520085.pdf.

6 "A Crisis of Ethics in Technology Innovation", Max Wessel, Nicole Helmer, *MIT Sloan Management Review*, 10 March 2020, https://sloanreview.mit.edu/article/a-crisis-of-ethics-in-technology-innovation.

7 The Theory of Moral Sentiments, Adam Smith, Lulu, June 2018, https://www.amazon.com/Theory-Moral-Sentiments-Philosophical-Psychological/dp/1387879987.

8 Wikipedia entry on *crony capitalism*, https://en.wikipedia.org/wiki/Crony_capitalism.

9 Wikipedia entry on *corporate welfare*, https://en.wikipedia.org/wiki/Corporate_welfare.

10 Wikipedia entry on *surveillance capitalism*, https://en.wikipedia.org/wiki/Surveillance_capitalism.

11 Grow the Pie: How Great Companies Deliver Both Purpose and Profit, Alex Edmans, Cambridge University Press, March 2020, https://amazon.com/Grow-Pie-Companies-Deliver-Purpose/dp/1108494854.

12 Conscious Capitalism: Liberating the Heroic Spirit of Business, John Mackey, Rajendra Sisodia, Harvard Business Review Press, January 2013, https://www.amazon.com/Conscious-Capitalism-Liberating-Heroic-Business/dp/1422144208.

[13] Doing Capitalism in the Innovation Economy: Reconfiguring the Three-Player Game between Markets, Speculators and the State, William Janeway, Cambridge University Press, May 2018, https://www.amazon.com/Doing-Capitalism-Innovation-Economy-Reconfiguring-dp-1108471277/dp/1108471277.

[14] Rethinking Capitalism: Economics and Policy for Sustainable and Inclusive Growth, Michael Jacobs, Mariana Mazzucato, Wiley-Blackwell, August 2016, https://www.amazon.com/Rethinking-Capitalism-Economics-Sustainable-Inclusive-dp-1119120950/dp/1119120950.

[15] Reimagining Capitalism in a World on Fire, Rebecca Henderson, PublicAffairs, April 2020, https://www.amazon.com/Reimagining-Capitalism-World-Rebecca-Henderson/dp/1541730151.

[16] Wikipedia entry on *punctuated equilibrium*, https://en.wikipedia.org/wiki/Punctuated_equilibrium.

[17] Grow the Pie: How Great Companies Deliver Both Purpose and Profit, Alex Edmans, Cambridge University Press, March 2020, https://amazon.com/Grow-Pie-Companies-Deliver-Purpose/dp/1108494854.

[18] Ibid.

[19] "Please, Please Buy This Gun Company", Andrew Ross Sorkin, *The New York Times*, 14 May 2018, https://www.nytimes.com/2018/05/14/business/dealbook/remington-bankruptcy-gun-safety.html.

[20] "In A Grain Of Golden Rice, A World Of Controversy Over GMO Foods", Dan Charles, *NPR The Salt*, 07 March 2013, https://www.npr.org/sections/thesalt/2013/03/07/173611461/in-a-grain-of-golden-rice-a-world-of-controversy-over-gmo-foods.

[21] "A Suicide, an App and a Time for a Reckoning", Kara Swisher, *The New York Times Opinion*, 25 June 2020, https://www.nytimes.com/2020/06/25/opinion/robinhood-suicide-trading.html.

[22] The Innovator's Dilemma: When New Technologies Cause Great Firms to Fail, Clayton M. Christensen, Harvard Business School Press, 1997, https://www.amazon.com/Innovators-Dilemma-1st-first/dp/B0076ZFPKW.

[23] How will You Measure Your Life, Clayton Christensen, James Allworth, Karen Dillon, Harper Business, May 2012, https://www.amazon.com/How-Will-Measure-Your-Life/dp/0062102419.

[24] The Power of Positive Deviance: How Unlikely Innovators Solve the World's Toughest Problems, Richard Pascale, Jerry Sternin, Monique Sternin, Harvard Business School Press, 16 June 2010, https://www.amazon.com/Power-Positive-Deviance-Unlikely-Innovators/dp/1422110664.

[25] Leadership and the New Science: Discovering Order in a Chaotic World, 3rd Edition, Margaret J. Wheatley, Berrett-Koehler Publishers, September 2006, https://www.amazon.com/gp/product/B00BYGU8S8.

[26] The Innovator's Dilemma, When New Technologies Cause Great Firms to Fail, Clayton Christensen, Harvard Business Review Press, May 1997, https://en.wikipedia.org/wiki/The_Innovator%27s_Dilemma.

[27] What Customers Want: Using Outcome-Driven Innovation to Create Breakthrough Products and Services, Antony Ulwick, McGraw-Hill Education, August 2005, https://www.amazon.com/What-Customers-Want-Outcome-Driven-Breakthrough/dp/0071408673.

[28] Business Model Canvas was developed by Strategyzer.com and is referenced under Creative Commons. See https://www.strategyzer.com.

[29] Business Model Generation: A Handbook for Visionaries, Game Changers, and Challengers, Alex Osterwalder, Yves Pigneur, John Wiley and Sons, July 2010, https://www.amazon.com/Business-Model-Generation-Visionaries-Challengers/dp/0470876417.

[30] Ibid.

[31] Democratizing Innovation, Eric Von Hipple, The MIT Press, April 2005, https://www.amazon.com/Democratizing-Innovation-Eric-von-Hippel/dp/0262002744.

[32] "Copycat: How Facebook Tried to Squash Snapchat", Billy Gallagher, Wired, 16 February 2018, https://www.wired.com/story/copycat-how-facebook-tried-to-squash-snapchat.

[33] Seeing Around Corners: How to Spot Inflection Points in Business Before They Happen, Rita McGrath, Houghton Mifflin Harcourt, September 2019, https://www.amazon.com/Seeing-Around-Corners-Inflection-Business/dp/0358022339.

[34] "How Facial Recognition Technology Leads To A Surveillance Society", John Torpey, Forbes, 21 May 2019, https://www.forbes.com/sites/johntorpey/2019/05/21/how-facial-recognition-technology-leads-to-a-surveillance-society/#43b17d315f68.

[35] "The world's scariest facial recognition company, explained", Rebecca Heilweil, Recode, 08 May 2020, https://www.vox.com/recode/2020/2/11/21131991/clearview-ai-facial-recognition-database-law-enforcement.

[36] "IBM's decision to abandon facial recognition technology fueled by years of debate", Hannah Denham, The Washington Post, 11 June 2020, https://www.washingtonpost.com/technology/2020/06/11/ibm-facial-recognition/.

[37] "Amazon Pauses Police Use of Its Facial Recognition Software", Karen Weise, Natasha Singer, *The New York Times*, 10 June 2020, https://www.nytimes.com/2020/06/10/technology/amazon-facial-recognition-backlash.html.

[38] Atomic Habits: An Easy & Proven Way to Build Good Habits & Break Bad Ones, James Clear, Avery, October 2018, https://www.amazon.com/Atomic-Habits-Proven-Build-Break/dp/0735211299.

[39] "#200 – Creatures of Habit: A Conversation with James Clear", *Sam Harris Making Sense Podcast*, 29 April 2020, https://samharris.org/podcasts/200-creatures-habit.

[40] "Marc Benioff: We Need a New Capitalism", Marc Benioff, *The New York Times Opinion*, 14 October 2019, https://www.nytimes.com/2019/10/14/opinion/benioff-salesforce-capitalism.html.

[41] "Sustainability as BlackRock's New Standard for Investing", Larry Fink, *Blackrock Client Letter*, 2020, Blackrock, https://www.blackrock.com/corporate/investor-relations/blackrock-client-letter.

[42] "Business Roundtable Redefines the Purpose of a Corporation to Promote 'An Economy That Serves All Americans'", Business Roundtable, 19 August 2019, https://www.businessroundtable.org/business-roundtable-redefines-the-purpose-of-a-corporation-to-promote-an-economy-that-serves-all-americans.

[43] "Council of Institutional Investors Responds to Business Roundtable Statement on Corporate Purpose", Council of Institutional Investors, 19 August 2019, https://www.cii.org/aug19_brt_response.

[44] "Dual-path Strategy", Brian Christian, presentation given at the *Innov8rs Unconference*, 29 July 2020, https://www.theinovogroup.com/dual-path-strategy.

[45] "Maximizing Profits: Milton Friedman", Open Textbooks for Hong Kong, 15 January 2016, http://www.opentextbooks.org.hk/ditatopic/19974.

CHAPTER 2

INNOVATION – BEWARE OF

THE DARK SIDE

Dr. Bettina von Stamm

I first shared my thoughts on the dark side of innovation, tentatively, in my Innovation Keynote at the 18th International Conference on Engineering Design in Copenhagen in 2011. Tentatively, as certainly then, if not still, innovation was considered to be the holy grail of everything that ails our world. Whether it is organization or governments, the call for innovation was – and is – resounding throughout the world.

To a degree rightly so. Whether it is a survey of 100 UK-based best practice companies by the British Department for Trade and Industry from 1995 that found that innovation was considered to be the most important differentiator[1], or a McKinsey article released June 17th 2020 in which they argue that, "Prioritizing innovation today is the key to unlocking post crisis growth". According to their research, 'through-crisis innovators' outperformed S&P 500 companies in the 2008/09 crisis by 10%, with the gap increasing to outperforming them by as much as 30% in 2013[2].

But... I do not use 'buts' lightly as I feel that in most instances they are not warranted. All they do is cause a negative atmosphere and dampen any fire or energy that might otherwise lead to something of value[3]. Yet when it comes to believing that innovation is the be all and end all, there has to be a firm 'but'.

While innovation – deliberate or accidental – is very important for shaping our future, and has been the driver of evolution for millennia, innovation must not become an end in itself, which I feel it has in many organizations. This is why in my nearly 30 years of experience in the field of innovation, there is no question that tends to upset senior leaders more than, "You say you want innovation, why?"

I feel very strongly that innovation has to have a purpose, and am concerned that in our quest for ever more innovation we seem to forget that where there is light there are shadows. While on the one hand innovation creates the light that illuminates the future not only for organizations but humanity, it also has the potential to create harm and cast deepest darkness.

My argument against 'buts'

I got sensitized to the impact of 'buts' in the particular context of innovation and idea management where there's nothing that sucks energy and enthusiasm out of a passionate person faster than the word 'but'. Who has not experienced the excitement of sharing an idea or suggestion just to be deflated in no time by the response 'interesting' or 'great' followed by 'BUT'. Once sensitized, I started to pay more attention to these three letters, noticing not only that we all seem to use them a lot, I also noticed there are only a few occasions when 'but' is truly warranted! "It is nice weather but I have to work." Is this really a contradiction or mutually exclusive, which the 'but' implies? How does it make you feel if you say "It is nice weather but I have to work", and how does it make you feel if you say "It is nice weather and I have to work"? Any difference? For me there is. One makes me depressed and annoyed with my work, the other makes me enjoy the beautiful sunshine and allows me to relish the blue sky I see when looking out of the window. The facts don't change, how I feel does!

The Dark Side of Innovation

Despite education's best efforts to drive it out of us, with inquisitive minds being labelled 'difficult', 'annoying', or 'slow in the uptake', curiosity and creativity are inherent in human nature. Humanity continues in its endless pursuit of knowledge and understanding, even those of us who do empathize deeply with the wisdom of the likes of Aristotle and Albert Einstein, who both realized that, "The more I learn, the more I realize how much I don't know."

Those who are curious and creative also tend to be passionate, pursuing their ideas with determination and doggedness; indeed, many innovations would never come to see the light of day without it. Yet it is that same passion, determination, and doggedness that leads the innovator to be excited by the possibilities, focusing on the positive outcomes, rather than also asking questions about potentially harmful applications or unintended consequences – only 0.2% of innovation studies look at the indirect consequences of innovation[4].

The fact is, once something has been invented, it cannot be 'un-invented'; Pandora's box is open.

Indeed, there are quite a few aspects that lead innovation to drift over to the dark side:

- Innovation that is lacking purpose.
- Too much innovation.
- Innovation that is released too soon.
- When good innovation turns bad.
- Innovation that goes a step too far.

I will explore all of the above in a little more detail below.

Innovation That Is Lacking Purpose

More men fail through lack of purpose than lack of talent.

Billy Sunday[5]

I believe that in Billy Sunday's quote 'men' could well be replaced with 'innovations'. Innovating because everyone else is doing it, innovation without direction, without a worthwhile purpose, is clearly a waste of valuable resources. Some may consider this to be one of a 'lighter shades of the dark side of innovation'. Yet in today's world, where the realization that we are living on a finite planet with finite resources is finally hitting home with more and more people, such innovation is irresponsible. I believe that purposeless innovation is not only wasting physical resources, it is also wasting employees' engagement, enthusiasm, and commitment, and thus undermines a willingness to engage in future innovation activities.

When you are innovating, do you ask about purpose? And if so, is the answer, 'satisfying customer needs'? Is it truly that, or is this masking the true driver, which is 'making money for our shareholders'? Can and should that really be the one and only driver? I believe that the purpose of innovation should be to create a future, for our children's children. This means innovation has to be a stepping stone towards a truly sustainable and worthwhile future. As a result the purpose of innovation should be to create value, and that 'value' should not only be monetary and give the shareholders their due, but satisfy all three aspects of the triple bottom line, the environmental and social, in addition to the financial.

If focusing on all three aspects of the triple bottom line sounds altruistic, think again. US-based investment manager BlackRock found that investment funds that track companies with better ratings on environmental, social, and governance (ESG) issues lost less money than those funds that track companies performing worse on ESG issues, in 94% of cases during the crisis[6].

Too Much Innovation

Too much of anything is bad, even the good can be a curse.

adjusted from singer Cheryl Cole

With this incredible choice of products and services, who has not looked at the offering and asked themselves, which product or service should I choose, and why? In 2015 there were 24,000 different Android devices alone in the market. I most certainly am one of those who likes to postpone purchasing decisions of electrical goods for as long as possible, as I find the offering overwhelming and confusing, with minute differences in existing models, and the promise of new, even better models around the corner. I feel that there is such haste in turning out more and more models that there is no time to actually reap the benefits of our previous efforts, maximizing our return on investment, which otherwise seems to be a top priority for all managers.

I recall the excitement with which a colleague talked about the advent of 5G and all the benefit it would bring. I could hardly contain myself as I am not even able to sustain a phone call on my train journey from King's Lynn to London (for orientation: Cambridge is the half-way point) as neither GPRS nor 3G or 4G are established sufficiently to facilitate that. Without any of these technologies fully supported (other than in big cities), they are already investing in the next generation? How many systems are to be supported in parallel? It seems that haste, not speed is the order of the day.

A second aspect is that many devices have many features that never get used. It seems that many of us are entranced and seduced by the 'more more more' when it comes to features – even though we might not use most of them. Perhaps allowing more customization and individual choice of features might be a better approach, which is definitely possible with today's design and manufacturing methods. It would also have the advantage that people might feel a little more attached to their products and might keep them a little longer before 'upgrading'. This is highly desirable as we produced 50 million tons of electrical and electronic waste in 2019[7], and as only 20% are recycled, contributing significantly to the pollution of soil, water, and air[8].

A third and final point I'd like to raise here is that in this race to bring out the next model, all we are generally doing is to pursue a better mousetrap. The potential for creating value and really making a differences – financially as well as for the consumer – lies somewhere else entirely. The Doblin Group, an innovation consultancy, has identified ten types of innovation clustered into three areas of focus: Configuration (Profit Model, Network, Structure, Process), Offering (Product Performance, Product System) and Experience (Service, Channel, Brand, Customer Engagement)[9]. Conducting research into where organizations focus their investments they found it to be firmly in the 'Offering' area. However, when looking for where innovation was generating returns, it was in the other two areas, 'Network', 'Profit Model', and 'Customer Engagement' in particular – by a significant margin. Is it not intriguing that those managers who are generally extremely concerned about costs and efficiencies seem to sanction innovation that does not create value and, hence, wastes resources? Is the battle for consumers' attention really won with more minor modifications and more functionality?

Of course, to seek alternatives and create step-change innovations requires significant investment of time and energy upfront, and that is something no one seems to have any more. We are lucky if we have enough time 'to do'; for most of us there is not time left 'to be', or to think. Yet highly successful people, such as Warren Buffett, the CEO of one of the largest companies in the US, declares to have spent 80% of his career reading and thinking?

Innovation That Is Released Too Soon

Good things take time.

Ovid

This leads neatly over to the next reason why innovation may slip over to the dark side: releasing things too soon, because it is possible. There are two aspects to this, the first is that not all consequences are understood at the time of release. Seeking for potential downsides and unintended consequences seems to be pushed to one side by the excitement of bringing something new into the world. When genetically modified food was first introduced, were implications and consequences truly understood? Or were they understood and willingly ignored? Do we not know from colonization what happens to native species if alien ones are introduced?

I am not saying that these things should not be launched, nor that all consequences can be anticipated in advance; I am saying though, that a conscious discussion and exploration should take place to ensure we understand all consequences as best as we can. In order to avoid wasting resources this should happen as early as possible, certainly before products or services are released. I believe in a crisis situation, such as the coronavirus outbreak of 2020, there is a particular tendency to cut corners and jump to conclusions – with the best of intentions, and the worst consequences.

The second is that the evolution of technology seems to have outpaced humanity's ability to keep up with it, morally, emotionally, legally. We fail to develop and innovate the context in parallel with the technological innovation. What do I mean by that? Take self-driving cars. The technology seems ready to proceed, yet what is the moral code for designing the algorithms that decided whether the car should protect its driver or the maximum number of lives? Or are we comfortable to leave such decisions also to the faster and faster evolving artificial intelligence?

Regulations, standards, laws – all these things lag behind the developments and possibilities of the digital world; other aspects of the systems, processes, and procedures by which we humans operate, remain in the analog world. Education and government are two critical aspects that come to mind immediately.

Of course, there are also some noteworthy exceptions. The UK-based RSA[10] (Royal Society for Arts, Manufactures and Commerce) realized that in order to be able to identify and pursue opportunities for sustainable policy change that will make a difference to people's lives, two things needed to happen. First, the complexity involved in understanding the bigger picture needed to be acknowledged, and second, any response to this complex and uncertain social context had to be flexible and iterative. They capture the essence of this approach as, 'thinking like a system, acting like an entrepreneur'[11].

Then there is also Estonia, which declared its intent to run the entire country like a start-up back in 2016. Yet these seem to be exceptions. On the whole, governments fail to keep pace, and seem unable to deliver what is needed to prepare and cope with the ever faster changing, complex context in which we live. Indeed, through our actions we seem to hasten the acceleration, ignoring the fact that the consequence of different parts of a system moving at different speeds is that, ultimately, the system breaks apart.

Complex, not complicated – why does it matter?

First of all, the complexity of a system is not determined by the number of its parts, but by the interactions and connections between these parts; both interactions and connections tend to be unpredictable and unknowable.

A complicated system we can understand if we study it, analyze it, and take it apart. What is more, based on its past behavior, we can predict and influence how it will behave in future.

In contrast, however long we study and analyze a complex system, however much insight we gain into its past behavior, we will not be able to predict how it will behave in future.

Whereas survival and success in a complicated system thrive in hierarchical structures, in order to succeed in a complex system, empowerment and delegation are of the essence. With this come several challenges:

1. Everyone needs to have the will to take responsibility, and ability to execute their responsibilities.

2. Leaders need to let go of a mindset of command and control and embrace a role of facilitator instead, providing direction, empowering, enabling, and delegating.

3. When surrounded by fast-paced change, the trick is not to join in but to observe and slow down – not to come to a still stand but keep moving slowly. Think about it: reacting from a stationary position requires some energy to get moving; moving too fast makes it difficult to change direction. It is moving at a gentle pace that allows us to adjust direction with ease and speed – while also having enough energy to process and reflect on what we observe. But swimming against the stream requires tremendous courage and deep confidence.

When Good Innovation Turns Bad

When good things go bad, don't go with them!

Elvis Presley

I would argue that the intention behind much, if not most, innovation is to improve the state of the world – whereby what constitutes an improvement is of course up for discussion. This section is about situations where something that was intentionally designed to move us onto the path of sustainability is perverted, and contributes to undermining it instead. Situations where the intended benefits are cancelled out by the negative effects, causing costs to outweigh benefits – that is, the costs when taking a systemic view, a view that considers the needs of all three aspects of the triple bottom line, rather than just the economic ones, at the individual or organizational level.

Let me give you an example of what I mean. On my train journey from Kings Lynn to London I pass fields of all sorts: potatoes, different types of grain, sunflowers, meadows with sheep and cows, and increasingly, fields covered in solar panels. While a very few also accommodate sheep, it seems that many will rely on spraying the fields with weed killers and other chemicals to make sure that nature does not interfere with the solar installation. I wonder what a holistic cost-benefit analysis would reveal. Though it can get even worse, I have come across examples where wooded areas were cleared in order to make room for solar plantations.

To me this is a scenario where good innovation turns bad: when something that draws on the strength and plentitude of nature, and was invented to bring us a step closer towards sustainability, is being used to destroy even more of nature. Is not enough land already taken up with buildings, roads, and other contraptions of concrete, steel, and glass? Is it really necessary to cover fertile land, land that, if not used for the production of food, could be used for the creation of biotopes, to re-build our woodlands and forest?

Rather than covering more of nature with man-made materials, we should think about how to cover more of these features with nature. It is encouraging to see that at least some countries are indeed embracing this thought, such as China's Liuzhou Forest City, Mexico's Smart Forest City of Cancun, and Malaysia's Johor Forest City[12]. I also love the fact that in 2008 Ecuador wrote nature's right to exist into its constitution[13], since 2018 Colombia's part of the

Amazon is afforded the same protection by the Columbian state as its citizens[14], in 2017 New Zealand acknowledged its Whanganui River as a living being[15], and in 2019 Bangladesh has afforded all its rivers the same rights as living beings[16].

It seems that solar plantations are motivated yet again by only one aspect of the triple bottom line, profit. Yet it does not have to be like that; to benefit from solar power plant we do not have to cover up more green fields. All it takes is an open mind, the willingness to push boundaries, and seek solutions that combine the best of all worlds rather than do what we have always done, thereby creating a compromise on the lowest common denominator.

An example that illustrates that covering green land with solar panels is not the only way to benefit from solar installations is from the UK-based company Solar Century. Solar Century were determined to contribute to the acceleration of adoption of solar power, at the same time realizing that relying on the investment of individuals was a major impediment to dissemination. They decided that if it were possible to create a solar offering in the form of a tax-deductible investment, things might change. Key challenge: in order to qualify as a 'bankable' asset the solar installation had to be independent of the rest of the building's structure – which meant the solar installation had to stay on the roof without being fixed to it! If there was a physical connection between roof structure and solar structure warrantee and maintenance would become contestable. Using wind modelling software they were able to design a structure and layout that would ensure that the tiles would stay in place through the aerodynamic load pushing it down alone; no fixings are required for the solar installation, even if it were exposed to the force of a one-in-a-hundred-year storm. Thus Solar Century were able to create an investment product that could be leased to any investment fund. It was possible only by looking beyond the product itself, even turning force that could be destructive, i.e. the wind, into something that supports the system.

I always wonder why no one has thought about the one infrastructure that's everywhere, generally 'free' from nature: roads. Why not cover all roads with solar installations? The shade provided for the cars would probably bring additional benefits of reduced air-conditioning. I guess I know the answer, it would require the collaboration of parties that have never thought about collaborating before, and then there would be the question of responsibilities when things go wrong…

It is not only solar panels where a focus on economic benefits has perverted original intentions. The food industry is a field brimming with examples where food that was meant to be healthy has been turned into the opposite, such as many a breakfast cereal or yogurt where the extraordinary amount of sugar that has often been added over time outweighs any intended benefits. I am reminded of the story of a soup manufacturer who was concerned about the loss in market share and declining product sales. Investigations revealed that, over time the wholesome ingredients had fallen prey to cost reduction exercises, to be replaced by cheaper, and less nutritious ingredients. Cost savings might be necessary, but not at the cost of destroying value.

There seems to be something about food and the potential for slipping over to the dark side... In our ambition to make food look good, make it easy to package, and preserve it for as long as possible, we have sacrificed its nutritious value. Research reveals again and again that levels of vitamins and minerals in our fruit and vegetables is continuously dropping. For example, between 1975 and 1997 the average calcium levels in 12 fresh vegetables dropped 27 percent; iron levels 37 percent; vitamin A levels 21 percent, and vitamin C levels 30 percent[17]. According to more recent research, another reason for reduced vitamin levels in crops are increased CO_2 levels[18]. Our food might adhere to standards and look pretty, yet in what really matters, nutrients, it is underperforms in alarming ways. Our solution: we buy expensive vitamins and other dietary supplements. Are we really making most of innovation's potential?

Innovation That Goes A Step Too Far

Mark my words — A.I. is far more dangerous than nukes.

Elon Musk[19]

Progress, the ultimate goal of humanity; innovation, the ultimate tool of progress. Or so it seems.

Let's take a step back and have a look at the meaning of the word 'progress'. According to the Cambridge Dictionary it means "movement to an improved or more developed state, or to a forward position". Implied in the word 'progress' is the assumption (or acknowledgement) that the status quo leaves something to be desired. So improving on it sounds quite nice and positive, doesn't it?

Where is the improvement expected to come from? There seems to be the firm belief that 'technology will save us', that it is technology that will be able to alleviate our fears and concerns, particularly in times of crisis, be it environmental, social, or financial.

Yet I believe that nothing could be further from the truth; technology is more likely to take us further away from ourselves, and deeper into anxiety. We may have more 'friends' than ever before, yet so many of us also feel lonelier than ever before. In 2015 The Independent wrote about a 'Loneliness Epidemic'[20], and in 2018 the UK government appointed a 'Minister for Loneliness'[21]. Perhaps we would take this more seriously if more people knew that social pain is as real a sensation for us as physical pain: researchers have shown that loneliness and rejection activates the same parts of the brain as physical pain[22].

Sure, technology makes our lives easier: calculators mean we don't have to struggle with maths; cars, washing machines, dishwashers, and electrical lawn mowers made physical chores easier. Navigation systems save us from having to read maps – and the (back-seat-driver) arguments that often go with it. The microwave saves us from having to cook our own meals. Are these things not great? They are, AND...

When making some purchases in the garden center last year the cashier asked me for something close to £180.00 I was puzzled; I had done the math and was expecting something closer to £80. Upon checking the bill it turns out that an item from a previous customer's price-check had been added to my bill. The person at the checkout would not have noticed. But even once the item was removed the total still did not seem right. Upon checking I spotted that the till, of course computerized, had multiplied £4.99 by 3 and arrived at £20. Interesting. Obviously a very special 'discount' had been applied. While the first mistake might have been pretty obvious, would you have spotted the second one or trusted the results provided by the computer?

What happens when we trust technology without questions, and follow instructions rather than using our senses and particularly common sense? Here are just a few examples from the world of SatNavs[23]:

- Following his SatNav without questioning, an American tourist drove all the way across Iceland for 5 ½ hours long journey instead of the under 30 minutes it should have taken to reach the hotel, which was in the opposite direction.

- A lorry overturned in a narrow, private country lane after following his SatNav down what was clearly a farm track.

- According to an article in the Telegraph back in 2009, "Figures show that last year satellite navigation systems were blamed for causing around 300,000 people to crash in Britain, while a further 1.5 million admitted performing sudden direction changes because they were following the device's directions."

It seems that we have taken leave of our senses, and trust technology more than we trust ourselves. I believe that whom and what to trust goes much deeper. There is a German saying that '*Kindermund tut Wahrheit kund*', meaning that children speak the truth. Yet it seems that this truth, felt deeply and intuitively by children, can be rather uncomfortable for the grown-ups, who rather dismiss it than deal with it. As a consequence is that we, from a very young age, learn to distrust the voice inside of us, losing that infinite source of wisdom. I can certainly recount occasions where by dismissing my inner voice I made decisions I came to regret later.

In the context of business I have observed that in most organizations 'hard facts and data' are required when making business decisions. Yet the most successful business people seem to balance these hard facts with a gut feel, with an inner voice. But are decisions well and truly based on facts, however much we pretend? I believe that we like to present ourselves as rational beings, yet when looking at the biggest decisions in our lives – marriage, purchase of a house, or even a car, these decisions tend to be fundamentally driven by our emotions. This is why I like to say that if we were to admit that we are deeply emotional beings, our decisions would become more rational as a consequence.

But I am digressing a little. Coming back to technology, and the wide-spread belief that technology will save us.

Perhaps that's understandable. Technology makes our lives easier. Calculators and computers relieve us of mental chores, and LinkedIn, Facebook, and dating site suggestions alleviate the struggles with emotional choices. By relegating these chores and choices to technology, over time, we lose our ability to perform these functions ourselves and are banished to a world where we become passive observers and followers of suggestions given to us by technology. It seems that rather than perceiving technology's output as instructions or guidance, we obey them like orders. We no longer need to deduce, analyze, and come to our own conclusions, it is a world where the answers are given to us, by Google or which other search engine we are using, in a couple of seconds, and we accept them, unchallenged. Yet "interacting cognitively with the environment" is, according to my hero, Fritjof Capra, a key characteristic of living systems.

Looking at the German word for 'progress', '*Fortschritt*', we do get a slightly different picture. '*Fort*' means 'away', '*Schritt*' means 'step', so literally translated '*Fortschritt*' means 'to step away'. A subtle and interesting difference: the English word invites us to consider what we are stepping towards, the German term what it is that we are leaving behind.

In essence, I believe that in our desire to progress we seem to have left some important things behind: our ability to read our environment; our connection with nature, and with it the understanding that we are an intimately linked and interwoven part of it. Indeed, one of the key insights that can be taken from the science of quantum physics is just that: everything is connected. I believe that if we continue this path of progress that relies (almost) entirely on technology, we will ultimately lose what makes us human.

We humans have a multitude of senses. Sight, hearing, taste, smell, and touch are the five traditionally recognized senses. The ability to detect other stimuli beyond those governed by these most broadly recognized senses also exists, including sensing temperature, pain, balance, vibration, and various internal stimuli[24]. I wonder how many senses we have already lost over the millennia.

Perhaps it is not surprising that indigenous peoples, relying on their senses rather than technology in their lives, often have amazing observational skills, and an ability to read and understand their environment that goes well beyond that of 'civilized' peoples.

Today's connectivity has led to an ever increasing, incessant bombardment of information through the ever increasing number of channels. While technology might help us sift through and manage this information flow, the sheer volume and frequency of new information diminishes our ability to move things from the short term to the long term memory. This means that we are losing our ability to learn and make connections[25], reversing one of the proudest moments of human evolution, acquired when the prefrontal cortex developed.

With an ever larger percentage of the population living in cities – from 55% of the world's population today and set to increase to 68% by 2050[26] – there is also a disconnect from nature, reflected in research findings of the British Nutrition Foundation (BNF) that one in ten 11 - 14 year olds does not know that carrots and potatoes grow underground, and 6% stated that dairy cows produce eggs. Understanding this disconnect from nature can perhaps partly explain the unbelievable disrespectful and harmful way in which we treat water, soil, and air.

How far are we willing to go?

What kind of modifications to body and mind should be acceptable? There are some no-brainers. Prostheses to replace lost limbs have been around quite some time – who cannot conjure the image of a wooden-legged pirate. A step up from that is supporting inert limbs with technology: exoskeletons designed to enable those with lower limb disabilities to walk upright, or an exoskeleton that augments human strength such as a machine called the 'Body Extender' which can lift 50 kg (110 lb) in each extended hand or an exoskeleton for soldiers to enable them to carry loads of 90 kg (198 lb).

Most of us modify our bodies. It might be because we would like to maintain or improve our health: fillings in our teeth, removing damaged body parts (tumors), supporting failing body parts (glasses, hearing aids), or even replacing damaged or lost body parts (teeth, prosthesis). Or we might do so to enhance our beauty by using make-up, wearing high heels, or dyeing our hair.

Are some of the recent technological developments that invite us to give up even more control representative of the next step of human evolution? In an article from 2015, NewScientist reported the invention of a 'human cruise control', developed and tested by Max Pfeiffer of the University of Hannover. All that was required was to attach electrodes to a person's legs, then use Bluetooth and a mobile phone. Based on signals from the phone the muscles were activated act without any conscious effort (or knowledge) of their owner. I think I would rather sleepwalk, where my unconscious guides my steps than allow some other person – or hacker – to decide which path I chose! It somehow reminds me of the animated movie, Wallace & Gromit – The Wrong Trousers.

From an evolutionary perspective, by progressing, are we moving forwards, or backwards? We are augmenting our eyes and ears, we are replacing our teeth, and some of us our limbs, dye our hair, wear high heels.

Ironically, while we seem to be merrily letting go of our cognitive and physical abilities, it is our ambition to construct robots and computers with ever increasing ability to read context, learn, make new connections, create, and even show emotions.

Clearly, technology has great benefits but... as not much in this world is about 'either or', I would encourage all of us, while embracing technology, not to let go of our senses, particularly not of our common sense! If for everything which in the past would have required the use of our body, our mind, our senses, there is a technology, an app, or AI, what then is left, and what then is it that makes us human?

Preventing a Slip Over to The Dark Side

I like to think that it is primarily a lack of awareness and a lack of conscious decision-making that causes innovation to slip over to the dark side, rather than malicious intent.

Here are some thoughts on how to keep the innovation in the light.

- Innovation that is lacking purpose – Make sure you ask, why you are innovating, and what the value is that you are seeking to create. Does it satisfy the needs of all three aspects of the triple bottom line, and if not, what is the justification for ignoring one or other? Ask this question not only at the outset but throughout the design, development, and implementation phases. Purpose should become the touchstone when innovating.

- Too much innovation – Are all the different models really adding value? Is it the best use of your resources? Are there other ways of offering your customers choice? Are fast, constant iterations really what works for you and your industry? Just because it works really well for the software, and many others, it does not have to be right for you. Just because everyone else is doing it is not a good enough reason; as I read on LinkedIn the other day, "Stop trying to keep up with the Joneses, they're broke!"

- Innovation that is released too soon – You might wonder how you should know when it's the right time, especially when everyone seems to be suggesting that '80% right' is sufficient. Though in my view this is more about avoiding what Margaret Heffernan calls, willful blindness[27]. Willful blindness occurs when "we could know, and should know, but don't know because it makes us feel better not to know." Yet, as Albert Einstein said so wisely, "Those who have the privilege to know, have the duty to act."

- When good innovation turns bad – This one has a lot to do with morals, ethics, and responsibility. Those who compose recipes for food know what is good and what is bad for us humans, and that, in most instances, anything in moderation is okay. We know that we have started to tap into solar energy in order to alleviate the burden our excessive use of fossil fuel is placing on the planet. Knowing that, how can we harm nature further in order to create 'clean' energy? How can authorities and local governments sanction such initiatives?

- Innovation that goes a step too far – This takes us even deeper into morals, ethics, and responsibilities. A huge challenge here is that many of the innovations with the greatest potential for harm also have the greatest potential to do good. A computer chip implanted in the brain has helped Ian Burkart, who had lost his ability to control or move his hands and legs due to a freak accident, regain control over his right hand.[28] Yet, as most of us have experienced at some point or other, anything that is digital can be hacked, manipulated, and altered. Cutting and pasting genes can be used to eliminate illnesses – or to create the 'perfect' human being.

In the end, whether innovation is a force for good, for nurturing and caring for our planet and all who live on it, or a dark force, that sets us on a path of the destruction of our planet and all who live on it, is up to the decisions we make, each and every one of us, every day, every moment.

What are you going to do to make innovation's light shine so brightly that there is no place for the dark side?

End Notes

1 "Competitiveness: Forging Ahead", Government White Paper, DTI Publications, HMSO, London, UK, 1995.

2 "Innovation in a crisis: Why itis more critical than ever", Jordan Bar Am, Felicitas Jorge, Eridk Roth, McKinsey & Company, 17 June 2020, https://www.mckinsey.com/business-functions/strategy-and-corporate-finance/our-insights/innovation-in-a-crisis-why-it-is-more-critical-than-ever?.

3 The excerpt in the box is from a blog article of mine in which I share more thoughts on 'buts', and the need for embracing paradoxes.

4 "pro-innovation bias / collateral debt obligations / negative consequences / indirect consequences / risk", Karl Eric Sveiby – in The Future of Innovation, Bettina von Stamm, Anna Trifilova, ed., Gower, 2009, https://www.amazon.com/Future-Innovation-Anna-Trifilova-dp-0566092131/dp/0566092131.

5 Billy Sunday was an American Clergyman (1862-1935).

6 "Investing in firms with better record on social issues pays, study finds", Jasper Jolly, The Guardian, 17 May 2020, https://www.theguardian.com/business/2020/may/18/investing-in-firms-with-better-record-on-social-issues-pays-study-finds.

7 "UN report: Time to seize opportunity, tackle challenge of e-waste", UN Environmental Programme, 24 January 2019, https://www.unenvironment.org/news-and-stories/press-release/un-report-time-seize-opportunity-tackle-challenge-e-waste.

8 See, for example: "3 Scary Effects Of E-Waste On The Environment And Human Health", Green Ewaste Recycling, https://www.gerecycle.com/3-scary-effects-of-e-waste-on-the-environment-and-human-health/.

9 "Ten Types of Innovation: The Discipline of Building Breakthroughs", Doblin, https://doblin.com/ten-types.

10 From the RSA's website: "The RSA was founded during the Enlightenment by William Shipley in 1754 with the first meeting being held at Rawthmell's Coffee House, Covent Garden, London. Shipley's belief that the creativity of ideas could enrich social progress was reflected in the diversity of awards offered by the Premium Award Scheme. For the first 100 years the Society encouraged innovation and excellence through this scheme in six areas – Agriculture, Manufacture, Chemistry, Mechanics, Polite Arts, Colonies, and Trade." Today their work focusses on supporting innovation in three major areas: creative learning and development, public services and communities, and economy, enterprise, and manufacturing.

11 "Outdated public services must empower people to achieve change", Ian Burbidge, RSA, 05 July 2017, https://medium.com/rsa-journal/outdated-public-services-must-empower-people-to-achieve-change-70d7c6a3f3f0.

12 "Forest Cities – Introducing New World Smart Cities", *smartcity*, 11 February 2020, https://www.smartcity.press/smart-forest-city-projects/.

13 "Ecuador Adopts Rights of Nature in Constitution", Global Alliance for The Rights of Nature, https://therightsofnature.org/ecuador-rights/.

14 "Columbia", The Amazon Conservation Team, https://www.amazonteam.org/colombia/.

15 "New Zealand river granted same legal rights as human being", Eleanor Ainge Roy, *The Guardian*, 16 March 2017, https://www.theguardian.com/world/2017/mar/16/new-zealand-river-granted-same-legal-rights-as-human-being.

16 "This country gave all its rivers their own legal rights", Sigal Samuel, *Vox*, 18 August 2019, https://www.vox.com/future-perfect/2019/8/18/20803956/bangladesh-rivers-legal-personhood-rights-nature.

17 "Dirt Poor: Have Fruits and Vegetables Become Less Nutritious?", *Scientific American*, 27 April 2011, https://www.scientificamerican.com/article/soil-depletion-and-nutrition-loss/.

18 "Vanishing Nutrients", Elena Sugia, *Scientific American Blog*, 10 December 2018, https://blogs.scientificamerican.com/observations/vanishing-nutrients/.

19 "Elon Musk: 'Mark my words – A.I. is far more dangerous than nukes'", Catherine Clifford, *CNBC*, 13 March 2019, https://www.cnbc.com/2018/03/13/elon-musk-at-sxsw-a-i-is-more-dangerous-than-nuclear-weapons.html.

20 "The Loneliness Epidemic: We're More Connected Than Ever – But Are We Feeling More Alone?", Rebecca Harris, *Independent*, 30 March 2015, https://www.independent.co.uk/life-style/health-and-families/features/the-loneliness-epidemic-more-connected-than-ever-but-feeling-more-alone-10143206.html.

21 "Britain appoints minister for loneliness amid growing isolation", Lee Mannion, *Reuters*, 17 January 2018, https://www.reuters.com/article/us-britain-politics-health/britain-appoints-minister-for-loneliness-amid-growing-isolation-idUSKBN1F61I6.

22 "The Pain of Social Rejection", Kirsten Weir, American Psychological Association, Vol. 43, No. 4, 2012, https://www.apa.org/monitor/2012/04/rejection.

23 "Sat Nav blunders 'have caused up to 300,000 accidents'", Aislinn Simpson, *The Telegraph*, 21 July 2008, https://www.telegraph.co.uk/news/uknews/2438430/Sat-Nav-blunders-have-caused-up-to-300000-accidents.html.

[24] You may want to read what an article by the World Economic Form has to say about this: "Humans have more than 5 senses", Alex Gray, World Economic Forum, 09 January 2017, https://www.weforum.org/agenda/2017/01/humans-have-more-than-5-senses/.

[25] See this video by Nicholas Carr for further reference: "What the Internet is Doing to Our Brains", Nicholas Carr, 06 May 2013, https://youtu.be/cKaWJ72x1rI.

[26] "68% of the world population projected to live in urban areas by 2050, says UN", United Nations Department of Economic and Social Affairs, 16 May 2018, https://www.un.org/development/desa/en/news/population/2018-revision-of-world-urbanization-prospects.html.

[27] Willful Blindness: Why We Ignore the Obvious at Our Peril, Margaret Heffernan, Walker Books, 2011, https://www.amazon.com/Willful-Blindness-Ignore-Obvious-Peril/dp/0802777961.

[28] "'Major milestone:' Paralyzed man regains control of hand", Wayne Drash, CNN Health, 14 April 2016, https://edition.cnn.com/2016/04/13/health/paralyzed-man-ian-burkhart-regains-control-of-hand/index.html.

CHAPTER 3

FOUNDATIONS OF

MORAL INNOVATION

Steve Wells

A New Day Arriving

There was a time (during the Industrial Revolution) when the titans of industry were focused on creating maximum profit, as energy technologies (fossil fuels and expanding electrification) enabled mass production of the materials and products needed to build the infrastructure and lifestyle of developing nations. Innovation was all about invention of the next time- and-labor-saving device and creating new ways to make things faster. "Build a better mousetrap and the world will beat a path to your door" was the popular saying. And it worked.

This was largely seen as a good thing and the titans – the 'Captains of Industry' – were well rewarded. In some cases, the wealth they acquired rivaled or exceeded that of the royals of the past. Workers were hired, people moved from farms to cities, the middle class was created, and consumer products were created for them. In this era, scant attention was paid to unintended or unanticipated consequences including pollution, urban blight, exploitive work practices, and deterioration of workers' health. Unions were a key factor in holding business owners to a higher ethical standard in the treatment of their workers. And conditions gradually improved.

Since that time, developed nations moved into the 'information economy' and working conditions correspondingly improved for employees. However, there was not a concerted effort to consider a larger purpose for the organization than the narrow business objectives of producing their specific products and services. Improvements in quality of life were essentially an accident of context rather than an altruistic motivation. An office is a cleaner environment, therefore healthier than a foundry or factory.

It is probably fair to say that we have reached a tipping point in the business of innovation. Recently the global population of Millennials surpassed that of their parents, the Baby Boomers. It has been widely reported that, as a group, Millennials have a desire to work for organizations that have a purpose greater than the bottom line. As reported on HuffPost.com[1], Generation Z, the cadre of youth following the Millennials and just entering the work force, are even more desirous of working for organizations that are socially responsible, human-centered, and ethical. This is in large part a reflection of the increased awareness of global issues, fostered by the internet, including for example, global warming, pollution, and human trafficking. Increasingly, organizations in both the public and private sectors are being held to higher standards. Though bad things are still done today, the days are largely gone when organizations can easily damage the environment or violate humans with impunity. Radical transparency and communication technologies that unite people of like-minded concern are creating an environment where organizations must consider public perception of their activities more than ever before.

But all is not well. Marc Benioff, chairman and co-CEO of Salesforce, in the 2019 New York Times article 'We Need a New Capitalism,'[2] stated that our current economic system "has led to profound inequality." Benioff continues, "To fix it, we need businesses and executives to value purpose alongside profit." Certainly, there is much work to do to convince the majority of business entities to pursue what has been called the 'triple bottom line' of People / Planet / Profit; the social, environmental, and financial aspects of an organization's impact. But a sea change has clearly occurred.

Neolatry

To listen to some, innovation is inherently better than what came before (it's easy to think of technology as values-neutral – it is just a thing). In the last century this has been a conclusion perhaps most frequently drawn by the Baby Boomer generation who were raised on dreams of automated homes, Jetsons-like space travel, and flying cars. This is what I term 'neolatry' (a portmanteau of 'neo' and 'idolatry') – the ultimate respect for, and near worship of, the 'latest and greatest.' Such neolatry has been a blind spot in the past, in the sense that the benefits of innovations have been touted without critique. Faster, stronger, brighter, higher, and so on is praised in utopian terms as if nothing unwanted could ever happen. Until it does. But by then the innovators are off to build the next great widget.

Today however, we have been seeing the negative consequences of innovations. In their book, <u>The Coddling of the American Mind</u> – a book about how young people are, even with good intentions, being over-protected from ideas to deleterious effects – Jonathan Haidt, a social psychologist, and Thomas Cooley, Professor of Ethical Leadership at New York University, cite the epidemic of depression and anxiety in young people that is fed, in part, by their obsession with social media and the natural comparisons they make with friends to whom they are connected. Those who created the various social media platforms certainly never saw that coming when they created these communication technologies. Their focus was undoubtedly on facilitating social and relational connections – a good thing. But the law of unintended consequences reared its ugly head.

There are many other examples that can be given. Plastic has been a beneficial material in manufacturing, from soda pop bottles to car dashboards, but it also has created a nightmare of waste in our landfills and oceans. Smartphones have many helpful capabilities, but divided attention while driving contributes to needless traffic accidents. Facial recognition technology can enable airport security to identify risks, but according to the work of Harvard social psychologist Shoshana Zuboff, it is also used for 'surveillance capitalism,'[3] in which the billions of photos uploaded to the internet are used to create profiles that enable companies to target and even manipulate the behavior of consumers without their knowledge – a threat to privacy. The list could go on.

Seeking a Footing

There are those who might argue for a values-free, objective pursuit of innovation, but this position is itself not free of value judgments. 'Values free' is a perspective valued by those who hold it. Typically, those who push this approach want things both ways: they are openly critical of values derived from past moral systems, while their own values escape the critical scrutiny they give others.

The move toward more values-focused business practices and ethical economies may all sound fine, but upon reflection one may begin to wonder where these values and ethics come from. In this book, the authors are pursuing the idea of a more moral approach to innovation. But this raises the question of what we mean by 'moral.' Where does that morality come from and who gets to decide what is moral and what isn't? There is usually little discussion about the foundation upon which some popular values are based. It is as if they are already accepted as a given. And the silence about these foundations may be masking a lack of agreement on values and their bases.

As a simple example, a brief look at the values behind the political parties in the United States reveals such lack of agreement. The right tends to favor equality of opportunity while the left tends to favor equality of outcomes. This is fairly obvious and not limited to the United States, but even within a political party, values are not a seamless cloth and there are sometimes sharp divisions. Small wonder that people speak of values in business and innovation in broad strokes. But it is not enough to throw out a general call for values-based business, government, and innovation as if everyone agrees on what the values are. Leaders and innovators won't know what values to pursue, or more likely, will uncritically mouth the 'flavor-of-the-month' values currently popular without someone specifying what values are worth pursuing and, more importantly, why they are.

With this being the case, a solution may be found in a review of the great religious traditions of the world. History, anthropology, and archaeology all attest to the fact that humankind have, in all places and eras, followed a religious impulse. Worship, faith, and morality in their various forms have been part of our collective experience since before recorded human history. Each of these traditions creates a community that offers a sense of belonging and social stability, and though each makes truth claims that contradict the others in significant ways, they all attempt to answer the 'ultimate' questions: Where did the world come from? Why are we here? What is the meaning of life? Why is there suffering and pain in the world? What moral behavior is required of me? Where do we go when we die? And so on.

Despite the presence of atheism, which has increased in popularity (albeit in comparatively small numbers) primarily since the period of the Enlightenment, people are still interested in and committed to values represented by these traditions. The supposed death of religion has been greatly exaggerated. Globally, it is not in decline. Without the foundation offered by religious thought the alternative is a system of right and wrong that is purely arbitrary. The religions of the world have always had at their root an understanding that their teachings are based on a foundation of revelation from a divine source, or at least a person with wisdom that surpasses that of the typical person.

This the not the place to debate the relative merits, let alone truth claims, of the world's religious belief systems. And in the present discussion doing so is not necessary for finding a foundation for moral innovation. For our purposes it will be enough to find the common ground in these traditions that will resonate with people around the world regardless of their faith orientation. It is this common ground which can form the basic skeletal structure of values that can guide innovators.

An excerpt about the values in different religions from The Abolition of Man by C.S. Lewis[4] is worth quoting at length:

> The Hebrew tradition talks of learning to separate the precious from the worthless. St. Augustine describes virtue as ordo amoris, or ordered loves, the wisdom to value things according to their worth. In Hinduism, there's the concept of Rta or the nature and supernature to which men's good conduct corresponds. The [Buddhists] talk about the Tao, a reality that is deep and rich beyond words, the greatest thing, preceding even the Creator. It's been called Nature or the Way or the Road. There are differences between religious and philosophical schools, but what they hold in common is significant: a doctrine of objective values, beliefs that some conduct is aligned with truth and others with falsehood. In this tradition from time immemorial, values and emotion are not at odds with reason, but join it in a glorious harmony.

Lewis was arguing the need for values in education, which had largely been the case prior to his writing, in contrast to calls for values-free education, and as stated above, such a view is not realistic as it has at its core its own set of values. It is in this vein that we see certain core values shared by the religions of the world as a foundation for moral innovation.

Timeless Values

Each religious tradition acts as the authority to guide people as to how they interact with both the physical world – what could be thought of as the horizontal relationship to both nature and people – and the spiritual world – what could be called the vertical relationship to the divine. In this role, each faith instructs and requires some behaviors while prohibiting others; in essence, the boundaries of morality.

An example of this comes from the Hebrew scriptures' ten commandments. The first four are about mankind's relationship to God (have no other [false] gods, keep the Sabbath, etc.) and the last six are about mankind's relationship to others (don't steal, commit adultery, murder, etc.). When quizzed by Jewish teachers of the law about the greatest commandment in the Torah, Jesus of Nazareth, the first century CE historical figure (and the reason it is called the first century) and founder of the Christian faith replied, "'Love the Lord your God with all your heart and with all your soul and with all your mind'. This is the first and greatest commandment." (the vertical), to which he added, "And the second is like it: 'Love your neighbor as yourself.'"[5] (the horizontal).

What then are the timeless values shared by these great religious traditions, followed by their faithful adherents for hundreds and even thousands of years? There are two primary categories of value in these traditions. First and foremost is the value and dignity of each person (though each faith values this in differing ways and degrees). One way this is seen is in the awareness of the spiritual world in a person's inner self and that this awareness is supremely important and something that elevates every person above the animal kingdom. Sikhism teaches this by saying that Heaven is within: ("Even as the scent dwells within the flower, so God within thine own heart forever abides."). The Judeo-Christian tradition ties human dignity to the origin story of mankind in the book of Genesis, in which God is revealed to say, "Let us make mankind in our own image..."[6]. It is this image of God, in every person, that confers dignity.

The Genesis passage goes on to say that part of being created in God's image is having purpose. After God created mankind, he gave them work to do and their work gave their existence meaning beyond mere survival.

In the religious traditions, human dignity requires humility and modesty, speaking truth and being a person of integrity ("Sincerity is the way of heaven, and to think how to be sincere is the way of a man." – Confucius). The Jewish scriptures have harsh words for those who make religious sacrifices but whose hearts are not in it and are just going through the motions. They also condemn those who arrogantly take advantage of the poor and politically weak. Similarly, in Jesus' famous sermon on the mount[7] he states that it is not enough to just follow the law outwardly, one must have an inward will to do what is right as well.

Another way dignity is seen is the proper proportion required between crime and its resultant punishment. In the Jewish code it was "an eye for an eye and a tooth for a tooth..."[8] This matching of the retribution or restitution to the severity of the wrongdoing maintained the dignity of both the party wronged: the punishment would be severe enough to recognize how much they had been harmed; and the wrongdoer: the punishment would not be overly severe.

The overarching dignity of humans is also seen in commands in all faiths (though expressed in various ways) for honoring one's parents[9], treating others as one would want to be treated themselves[10], service to others, compassion and generosity, especially to the poor[11], doing no harm to others, respecting others' property, not judging others but forgiving them and being slow to anger ("He who holds back rising anger like a rolling chariot, him I call a real driver; others only hold the reins." – Buddha). Jesus also taught the superiority of a life of love for others and that this love would be the motivating power behind right behavior. Interestingly, all major faiths teach respect for, and cooperation with, people of other faiths.

With these guidelines in mind, we can easily envision the sorts of innovation that would reinforce and advance the dignity of people everywhere. Innovations that provide them with meaningful work, educate them, end hunger, disease, war, crime and poverty, and that reduce the stresses and difficulties of life while adding beauty and joy are, in effect, doing God's work here on earth.

A second major area of moral values is stewardship of, or care for, the planet. Part of the dignified work God gave man, in the Judeo-Christian tradition, is being those who oversee and cultivate nature. A great evil was realized many years ago, specifically, ravaging the earth for its wealth with no regard for what remained. Strip mining is an example where the beauty of the land was destroyed in an effort to gain the value hidden beneath. This was performed in the most cost-efficient way regardless of other concerns like animal habitat or the balance of nature. We are more aware today of the consequences of the choices being made by business and government and there are calls for accountability and consideration of the 'circular economy' where any anticipated negative consequences are mitigated and, if possible, eliminated.

In 1990, the Dalai Lama said, "Our ancestors viewed the earth as rich and bountiful, which it is. Many people in the past also saw nature as inexhaustibly sustainable, which we now know is the case only if we care for it."

Part of stewardship of the planet means that in spite of the inherent dignity of humankind, it should not take such a place as to eliminate care for other forms of life and there is a deep concern for plant and animal life as well.

One aid in stewardship of the planet that enhances humanity's sense of dignity and purpose is education. Many religious traditions emphasize learning, not just about the divine, or one's moral responsibilities, but also about the world. A Jewish religious leader is called a rabbi, which means "my teacher," and their function is more about study and teaching what they have learned than performing rituals. It has been shown that education is a key to ameliorating poverty, raising the prospects of girls and women, exploring nature's mysteries, and creating the innovations that can make for a better world. This too is part of stewardship of our planet.

The universe was born out of the chaos of the primordial soup. Part of our care for the world is to press order into the chaos that remains. There are thousands upon thousands of ways in which the world and society is broken. As innovators pursue solutions, a sense of the dignity of purpose in working for a better world ennobles our efforts. There are several ways the religious traditions explain the brokenness, but all would agree that fixing it is a good that should be pursued. In this way we can emulate the great religious leaders who taught and modeled servant leadership. Jesus was a prime example of this and said it is "more blessed to give than to receive."[12] Innovators who view themselves as those who serve mankind, rather than as rulers over mankind, demonstrate the appropriate stewardship of creation.

Limits of Moral Responsibility

Assuming that the reader is still with me at this point, the questions might be raised, "What about an innovation that is conceived with all the best intentions to live up to the high standards of morality – pursuing the dignity of people, taking care of the planet, fostering education, meeting real needs – and is then 'released into the wild?'" How can an innovator ensure that an innovation is used with the good intentions with which it was created? As some of the co-authors here have said, the answer, in short, is: you can't. The technology that enables us to watch a Disney or Hallmark movie also enables people, children included, to access pornography. Clearly, the responsibility for moral intent and behavior, while shared by innovators, ends for them where their work ends. We can't be moral for others – they own that responsibility. We, as innovators, should consider outcomes and try to anticipate harmful, unintended consequences, but human history has shown that even with good laws (which is, of course, part of the answer) people will, for their own misguided reasons, violate those laws and do what our religious traditions say we should not. There is no way to prevent the evil perpetrated by others from happening. Everyone is a moral free agent and responsible to choose to do what is right.

As innovators, we can only take positive action where we have control. And there are certainly many opportunities to do so. As an example, innovators can work to ensure that their innovations are beneficial for all people and not just the moneyed elite. We will likely have to be explicit and perhaps even forceful at times to increase the likelihood of that outcome. And if we can, we should.

Innovation, by definition, operates at the frontiers of knowledge and human experience. As such, there are often no specific established rules for what the ethical thing to do is. Ethics tends to be a responsive, and therefore lagging, discipline. With that as the de facto context of innovation, it becomes incumbent on the innovators to anticipate where the ethicists will land (self-educating on the topic would help) and let their expectation of future determinations of right and wrong guide their choices. The two main thrusts of moral agreement among the great religious traditions of the world, doing good to our neighbors due to their inherent dignity, and stewardship care of the planet, are the best starting points for that guidance.

End Notes

1 "Think Millennials Are Purpose-Drive? Meet Generation Z", Zach Mercurio, *Huffpost*, 28 November 2017, https://www.huffpost.com/entry/think-millennials-are-purpose-driven-meet-generation_b_5a1da9f3e4b04f26e4ba9499.

2 "Marc Benioff: We Need a New Capitalism", Marc Benioff, *The New York Times Opinion*, 14 October 2019, https://www.nytimes.com/2019/10/14/opinion/benioff-salesforce-capitalism.html.

3 The Age of Surveillance Capitalism: The Fight for a Human Future at the New Frontier of Power, Shoshana Zuboff, *PublicAffairs*, 15 January 2019, https://www.amazon.com/Age-Surveillance-Capitalism-Future-Frontier/dp/1610395697.

4 The Abolition of Man, C.S. Lewis, Macmillan, New York, 1947, p. 6, https://www.amazon.com/Abolition-Man-C-S-Lewis/dp/0060652942.

5 Matthew 22:37-39, The Bible.

6 Genesis 1:26, The Bible.

7 Matthew chapters 5-7, The Bible.

8 Exodus 21:24, The Bible.

9 2:211, The Koran.

10 Jainism: Acarangasutra 5.101-2 (seen in various forms in 14 world religions).

11 64:16, The Koran.

12 Acts 20:35, The Bible.

CHAPTER 4

<u>INNOVATION ITSELF IS AMBIVALENT</u>

Mick Simonelli

Because innovation and creativity reside within the controls of flawed humans and organizations, it is ultimately impossible to create new innovation that understands, and works within, the boundaries of what is beneficial to all of society, the world, and time. Innovation itself is ambivalent.

Innovation, as wonderful and positively powerful as it is, is also a powerful force for destruction and negativity. In fact, every innovation is subject to the yin and yang of the individual, society, and the world; and there are as many negative uses of innovation as there are positive. Even the mere terms positive and negative are value-loaded, because what is positive to one person or society could be negative to another. So, while, for example, life-changing 3D-printed prosthetics or certain genetically-modified foods may be positive, it remains that those very same innovations could in fact be used for equally negative outcomes.

The splitting of the atom is a classic example of the duality of innovation. It was a monumental achievement that changed the course of history for both good and bad. Yet, from its origin it possessed both great good and great evil. The most profound original application of the splitting of the atom was the atom bomb deployed during World War II, where the Manhattan Project organized a who's who of the smartest minds in order to collectively bring their theories to fruition. Oppenheimer, Einstein, and a whole host of the most highly respected physicists in the world came together to split the atom. The very methods they used are still in use today across the world. Called 'skunk works'®[1], it is a proven method for detaching cross-functional teams to create disruptive innovations, and it is still an effective innovation method in use today. In retrospect, was the splitting of the atom good or bad?

Historians will disagree whether that original usage was good or bad, positive or negative. Certainly, from an American or Allied World War II perspective, it was positive because it won a very bloody war. But the very same usage was extremely negative for the Japanese and her Allies; and not only ended their war chances but also had very costly civilian casualties.

Since that initial usage, nuclear fission has been deployed for a wide range of new innovations including x-rays, cancer radiotherapy, satellite power, and of course nuclear reactors. Nuclear reactors have proven to be one of the most reliable energy sources on the planet with over 10% of the world's energy deriving from nuclear power, and an estimated 30% of the users would not have reliable electricity without it.[2] These are clearly positive outcomes.

Yet, if we examine the usage of nuclear plants from an environmental perspective, it is not so good. Nuclear waste that comes from those nuclear power plants and nuclear weapons is a worldwide hazard. The waste is persistent and toxic to almost every living thing. The disposal of that waste is a generational issue that continues to worsen. Even if one argues that nuclear plants are a positive force for electricity generation, one must also acknowledge that the resulting radioactive waste is a very significant negative. One can easily see the dichotomy of innovation uses and outcomes within just this one global innovation of atom-splitting.

An even worse outcome of the atom-split is the proliferation of nuclear weapons around the globe. For the first era in human history, self-destruction of the human race is a possibility… a not-so-insignificant outcome of the atom-splitting innovation. Nuclear weapons are known to be owned by China, the United Kingdom, France, Israel, Pakistan, India, and North Korea. Combined, there are an estimated 15,000 nuclear weapons worldwide (that we know of). This is enough to destroy everything on the planet a hundred times over.[3] Not to mention the nuclear winter that would follow. It would be an extinction of the planet unlike anything ever imagined possible. And… the utter annihilation of the earth would be… DIRECTLY TRACEABLE… to the atom-splitting innovation.

Another complicated practical example is the development of modern medicine cures for just about everything that inflicts mankind. From chicken pox to malaria to the measles, the last 100 years of medicinal inventions have been remarkable. According to the U.S. Census Bureau, the average life expectancy at the beginning of the 20th century was 47.3 years. A century later, that number had increased to 77.85 years thanks in large part to advancements and innovations within medicine. Organizations are even taking on the dreaded heart disease and cancer with increasing success.

In fact, for skin cancer (melanoma), a large biopharma company has even found what has tested out to be a cure for melanoma skin cancer. That's right, a cure for skin cancer. In recent tests they have received a 50% plus cure rate for the worst stage 4 cancer patients. But here is the rub, and the gray area, of some medicinal innovation, the treatment costs about $500K and isn't currently covered by any U.S. insurers. That means that if a skin cancer patient doesn't have the money to pay for the cure, they may die (even though a cure is immediately available).

So why doesn't someone, the government for example, force the biopharma company to lower their prices? Well, it's not that simple. The biopharma company has spent tens of millions of dollars and other resources that they must recoup in order to stay viable. So while the price is currently exorbitant, if society wants to keep incentivizing biopharma to develop more cures, they must be allowed to recoup their costs and even make a profit. The good and evil here is in the details of the deployment of the product and how it I used. It would be so wonderful to provide the drug treatment freely to everyone with melanoma skin cancer, but if that were done then the company would go out of business. Tremendous good is occurring as a result of this innovation, but unfortunate side effects of non-treatment are also occurring.

While these historical and practical examples definitely point to the good and evil duality of uses for innovations, the author of this chapter has been the inventor of innovations that are ambivalent as well. As a former Army Transformation Officer, my very first innovation was a weapon system called the SLAMRAAM (shown in the photo of **Figure 3** below) that was developed by myself, an Air Force partner, and some motivated defense contractors. Used for tactical air defense, its purpose was to shoot down enemy aircraft before they could attack friendly forces. Now deployed around the world in various armed forces, it has been effective in protecting ground troops from aerial attacks. The SLAMRAAM is a very positive thing if you're one of those ground troops. Yet, if you happen to be the other force receiving a missile up your tail-pipe, it's a very negative thing. Again, we can see that innovations can be good or bad, depending on your perspective and their use. One that I personally experienced frequently while in the Army.

Figure 3: SLAMRAAM in action.

We have seen that there are clearly some innovations that are more inclined to be used positively, and some that are more inclined to be used negatively. Most noteworthy innovations are ambivalent – used for both great good and great harm. The ethics of innovation and of the humans who create and use them through time, are far too complex to ever be pigeon-holed into a solely positive impact. Those theories that ignore the ambivalence of innovations are not valid theories at all, but are nullified by an unbiased examination of innovation history as evidenced by some of the examples given in this chapter. In this hyper-innovation environment, many argue that we are at an inflection point in human history where our inventiveness and creativity must be used only for good. But the truth of our existence and history of innovation refutes that belief. Innovation is not a holy grail for goodness, but instead is a powerful and wonderful tool that can be used for both good and evil.

End Notes

[1] "Skunk Works®" is a registered trademark in the United States of Lockheed Martin Corporation.
"Skunkworks®" is a registered trademark in Australia of The Novita Group Pty Ltd.

[2] "18 Advantages and Disadvantages of Nuclear Fission", Keith Miller, *Future of Working: The Leadership and Career Blog*, https://futureofworking.com/6-advantages-and-disadvantages-of-nuclear-fission/.

[3] "What If We Blew Up All The World's Nukes at Once?", Kyle Mizokami, *Popular Mechanics*, 01 Apr 2019, https://www.popularmechanics.com/military/weapons/a27008390/blow-up-every-nuke/.

CHAPTER 5

THE FUTURE IS CONSCIOUS – AND ORGANIZATIONS MUST MODEL THIS HUMANIZING PRACTICE TO PROSPER

Michael Graber

A Vision of Innovation Leading a Global Movement

Ever since Homo Sapiens rose from the evolutionary petri dish, the ability to innovate has set us apart from other species. Most of our markedly Human accomplishments – from language development, hunting prowess, adoption of complex tools, agriculture, aqueducts, transportation, to space travel, the internet, sequencing DNA, and military and medicinal breakthroughs – have empowered giant leaps in our collective quality of life, safety, and collective protection.

Now, given three, prolonged global crises: the ravishes of climate change, the humanitarian crisis that produces so many refugees, and the crisis of truth and meaning (just watch several news channels for evidence), our species stands at an inflection point. This significant call-to-action asks us to rise to face the seemingly insurmountable challenges and redeem ourselves, the planet, and other species to whom we are connected.

This calling requires a reorientation of our values, talents, and innate proclivities. So much of our lens for seeing the world is based in 19th and 20th Century ways of seeing the world. The old boundaries of tribe, nation, and religion will need to shape-shift to allow an inclusive view that sees the lesson we learned with splitting the atom: we are all one. More important, we cannot allow Classism to separate us from treating every single person with respect and humility.

We passed the apex of the Industrial Revolution in the 1990s. Given trends in nanotechnology, gene editing, and global issues, it's impossible to manage the new world with the mindset of the old world.

Yet, most MBA schools still teach a single-minded shareholder profit motive as its prime mover and template. This paradigm colors every aspect of management and leadership judgment and behavior. As one example, take the term Human Resources – thinking of people as resources, replaceable cogs in a machine, comes directly out of Taylor's Scientific Management theories of optimization.

Take the field of Marketing as a second example. Even the way we dehumanize potential users of our products and services is objectifying: B2B or B2C.

Yet, the world is surfeited with too much junk made for the too simple reason of making money. The oceans are filled with our junk and our landfills are at capacity.

Corporate Innovation can play a leading role in this transformation. Smart organizations know that they prosper best by creating products and services that fit an actual need, creating no waste.

Now, what if we take the same methods – Design Thinking, Lean, Jobs to Be Done, etc. – and turn our inherent better nature on solving the vexing crises of our time?

This is our movement, our inspiration, and our calling. Join us as we use Innovation to make the world a healthy place for each of us to thrive and reach our potential.

The real disruption is that organizations are waking up to realize they are not a monolithic entity – and that culture is a very human phenomenon. This awakening in accelerating the heart of the post-industrial world, the emerging human-to-human era. It's an era led by compassion and backed with helpful zeal.

Business Becomes More Human

An R&D scientist said to me, "we need to always begin new product development projects this way," after sifting through 20+ in-depth consumer narratives of their condition. These people went into great details about their lives, their struggles, their rituals, their beliefs. As we unpacked their learnings the scientist understood the complexities of having a rich, full contextual understanding of the people for whom he will design new, innovative solutions. To summarize with a metaphor, he walked in their high heels, sneakers, and Crocs, embodying their situation as if it were his life own.

Instead of creating another barely distinguishable product from the sea of sameness that surfeits the shelves of food, drug, and mass stores off of a job brief that solves a marketing line problem, this scientist can now collaborate on a new approach to these problems with a deep understanding of the situation.

The insight at hand is that we are not solving business problems here. We are solving human problems. In this era when landfills and the seas are gutted with enough plastic to choke the planet, do we really need another product for the sake of making money solely? Wouldn't it be better if we create things people need, people use, and that help people? Please do not tell me that this is idealistic.

This is the business-world paradigm shift of our era. Forget business-to-business. Forget business-to-consumer. That is outdated thinking.

We are crafting solutions for real people. Instead of creating a me-too product for an ambiguous market segment, real innovations seek to connect with the fate and fabric of their users' lives. This is human-to-human business and smart product design, part cause-based, and part entrepreneurial horse sense, but it makes business good and it also, no surprise, makes good business.

Following this human-centered process, Design Thinking begins with empathy for real people. Later, product ideas are co-created with real people. This hand-on-the-pulse method creates new, breakthrough products and services that make a positive difference in the lives of many.

As the scientist says, "we need to always begin new product development projects this way." Welcome to the new era.

The Real Benefit of Design Thinking

Many days I catch myself uttering "thank you" to the universe, which the mystic Meister Eckhart claims is a prayer sufficient enough to carry an individual through an entire life.

Unlike a policeman or a bartender, I have the radical blessing to work in-depth with people doing inspiring exercises, which bring out the best side of their humanity. Being human is an incredible birthright. Our senses, instincts, and capacity for wonder can evoke awe upon contemplation.

Helping organizations create empathy with the people for whom they design solutions means being totally present with the widest cross-section of humanity imaginable. Given the variety of clients, we have the privilege to meet a lot of people – from soldiers to housewives, chemists to poets, wealthy to subsistence-level poor, athletes, butchers, warehouse workers, doctors, CEOs, you name it.

Typically, the more you constructively engage people with creative endeavors, in an air of respect, they open up. The trade term is Empathy; however, Empathy is such a clinical-sounding phrase. How about Humanizing instead of Empathy?

Then, there is co-creation, where we bring in groups of people to help us refine prototypes. Typically, there are three-to-six sessions with groups of six-to-ten people per project.

Here is what we have learned. If you sincerely ask someone for feedback and to help you make something better, they give it their best 99% of the time. One such humanizing moment is when one participant voices a problem or condition and the others focus intently on creating something for their new friend. People, when brought into community, genuinely want to help others.

The concepts get humanized. The people are respected for who and what they are, and are not mere two-dimensional marketing targets, and therefore are humanized. The brand or company for whom we are working becomes more in touch with the real people for whom they are designing solutions – organizational humanization. The whole process is humanizing.

The real benefit – the gift – of doing design thinking for a living is that the navigator of the project gets an immersive humanizing experience every day – and gets to make a living helping people discover their drives, passions, dislikes, and helping people articulate these esoteric responses to real things such as products, services, and experiences, and learn deeply from them.

As well, if you do this work day-to-day you know beyond a shadow of a doubt the essential oneness of people.

Despite the colors and flavors of culture, race, and ethnicity, people are people. I hold a long-standing conviction that many people harbor latent prejudices. Most tend to go through life with a filter of 'us' and 'our way' and 'other.'

Doing design thinking is a cure for such small mindedness – and is the real, lasting benefit of this humanizing work.

How to Thrive in the Emerging Human-to-Human Era

If you want to create products and sell them to people, well – to be blunt – nobody cares. The mass-market engine that drove this mode of production and type of selling has expired.

According to AcuPoll[1], more than 95 percent of new products fail each year. This harrowing statistic should sound an alarm, one that says the way we approach the conceptualization and launch of new products does not work.

Every year, billions of dollars shrivel down to zero. Careers and jobs are lost. So much talent and energy gets wasted in the misdirected compulsion to have something new.

In reality, the world doesn't need new stuff just because it is new. Landfills and aftermarket discount stores are filled beyond capacity. New doesn't equal net new growth. All new, in fact, is not created equal. New for the sake of having something new to sell is the most short-sighted, non-strategic, and unthinking mode of behavior for a company.

Here's the crux of the issue: if you want to create products and sell them to people, well – to be blunt – nobody cares anymore. The mass-market engine that drove this mode of production and type of selling has expired, hence the 95 percent failure rate. Don't create products for a too-general target and hope to push them.

Somewhere in the lust to create new value the most important factor in a successful equation was overlooked: the real people who may use your product. These humans, not objects to which you move a unit, but flesh-and-blood with the power to purchase, naturally desire a better life. If you create with them as part of your process, your success potential becomes much, much greater.

But new products that meet a real need for real people; well, that's something useful and novel – a product with distinction and different than the rest of the heap. Just ask Swiffer, users of Dr. Scholl's kiosk, or any other leading brand that keeps their consumers at the heart of the innovation, product development, and marketing efforts.

The trick: find people for whom you can solve problems. Then, get to know them deeply. Hang out in their homes, at their work, go shopping with them. Understand their rituals, their motivations, their relationship to the world and things in it. Know the people for whom you are creating.

Know also where the trends are pointing a few years out. Think about it in reverse. If you look back five years ago, half the people you knew didn't have Smart Phones, most had never stayed in an Airbnb or taken an Uber to their destination. Now, they use their phones to book these services and do so much more. Trends and technology are accelerating at a quantum speed.

If you want to be in the product business make it your business to know where culture, the market, and the world will be in two-to-five years. Product development can take a year or two, so make sure you are creating for how your people may be interacting with the world a few years out.

People matter to the success of your new products. Ignore them at your own risk. If you can add value to their life, you thrive.

If not, goodnight.

The Rise of Conscious Innovation

Business itself is morphing. Technology has met customer preference and disrupted many categories. Think of Airbnb, Lyft, and Uber, as well as UberEats. Look at the unimaginable growth of Apple and Amazon. Examine, too, the function of innovation as a formal discipline and the rise of Conscious Capitalism.

Here is what we are learning. Corporations that have consumer-driven innovation programs outperform their competition that relies on an outdated model of R&D to generate new value. Companies focused myopically on short-term value and a single profit motive only do less well than companies who embrace the emerging paradigm of Conscious Capitalism. According to a 10-year study, these Firms of Endearment (the title of book about the study[2]) outperform their peer companies eight-to-one while making a positive social and planetary impact in the world. Patagonia, Ben and Jerry's, and Middleby Corporation are examples of such companies.

This human-centered approach to commerce and its empowering dynamism in both the field of Innovation and the construct of Conscious Capitalism[3] make them different dimensions of the same profound shift. Business is changing, for the better. Instead of the sole goal of making money, it now wants to make money while creating significance and social value.

Those in the innovation field intuitively know that the main four tenets of Conscious Capitalism inspire their output more than corporate dictates for 'more quick wins.' In truth, they will tell you that by doing innovation sincerely the transformation that takes place within an organization – and the change management that ensues as a result – provides an inspiring purpose that it may have lacked under the previous model of value creation.

A **higher purpose** is also the first tenet of Conscious Capitalism. Speaking from our collective experience at the Studio, we are hesitant to take on a new innovation client if they are unwilling to tether their innovation strategy to a higher purpose. The reason is clear – it motivates the efforts and serves as a point of genuine pride helping to tap the highest potential of each professional involved in the effort.

The second tenet is **stakeholder integration** – rethinking the shareholder orientation to include all types of shareholders; not only investors, but also suppliers, the community, the employees, etc. While some companies may not stretch to this lofty goal in their corporate governance, once we do the Empathy and Co-Creation work there are always several conceptual solutions that incorporate a mode of giving back to the community as part of the total value it creates.

The third tenet of Conscious Capitalism is **conscious leadership**. Take my word for it: no true innovation will launch if you have executives who just give lip service to the effort. Innovation is a litmus test of conscious leadership.

Lastly, the fourth tenet of Conscious Capitalism is **conscious culture and management** – and nothing makes a culture more conscious than setting up innovation. Like a flashlight in the darkest corners of the organization, innovation uncovers every orthodoxy and demands a conscious response.

Practicing Innovation: An Inside Job

It is a heroic adventure being an innovation practitioner. To lead an organization to where it is ready to flex its culture, business model, practices, and management style requires the types of talents and skills that only metaphors can describe: the hunting instincts of a lion, the fortitude of a buffalo, the wisdom of an owl, and the patience of a turtle.

These extra-ordinary senses indicate how much you will be challenged and tested inside your own organization. Don't lose heart: it's part of the experience.

Indeed, if you are creating new ways of making money you will be seen as a threat to the Reign of Sameness. Given all of the internal forces actively (albeit sometimes unconsciously) working toward the failure of our work, you need these super-human powers.

You also need to remember that the practice of innovation is an inside job and takes devotion, passion, and clarity to excel. Here are some tips on the inside aspects of being an innovator.

Purpose. You need to be the type of person who is driven by purpose. This purpose-based mindset will provide you the confidence to not respond to criticism, the willpower to successfully compete to keep projects alive, and the inspiration to encourage and empowers others to meet your goals.

Purpose helps weather storms and hurdle barriers. Purpose is a deep well of potential, too often untapped by those in the corporate and non-profit worlds.

Quiet. If you spend every second reflexively responding to organizational stimuli, your head will fill with noise. You won't be able to think deeply or critically. You won't be able to create any new thinking. You won't be able to hear insights and concepts with a generative mind. Without finding that "moment in each day that Satan cannot find," as the poet William Blake so eloquently described silence, you will never escape the death-by-email-and-power-point plague that keeps real work from getting done.

As I told some friends once, take a few moments each day to look at insights, concepts, and business cases without judgment, without bias, without imposing the burden of the past onto them. If you have to trick yourself by looking them as if a different organization would launch them, do it. You cannot do this type of work without getting in that pensive, contemplative, introspective quiet place.

Curiosity. This quality may be the most critical inside-job quality of successful innovators. If you are not blessed with a rabid, insatiable, and systemic curiosity, you may be in the wrong field. Curiosity is the secret weapon of innovation, enabling connections that are not normally made, a questioning of orthodoxies that prohibit growth.

There is very little written on this core innate skill and its value in the workplace; however, it is how new value gets created. It's the taproot of empathy, defining problems, ideation, and market validation – all of the core skill sets of the innovator.

To thrive, Innovators need to be driven by purpose, spend some quiet time each day thinking deeply, and be afflicted with undying curiosity.

End Notes

[1] "New, improved ... and failed", Laurie Burkitt, Ken Bruno, *Forbes.com* on *NCBNEWS.com*, 24 March 2010, http://www.nbcnews.com/id/36005036/ns/business-forbes_com/t/new-improved-failed/#.XxDMTChKjIU.

[2] Firms of Endearment: How World-Class Companies Profit from Passion and Purpose, Rajendra S. Sisodia, David B. Wolfe, Jagdish N. Sheth, Wharton School Publishing, 2007, https://www.amazon.com/Firms-Endearment-World-Class-Companies-Passion/dp/0133382591.

[3] Conscious Capitalism: Liberating the Heroic Spirit, John Mackey, Rajendra Sisodia, Harvard Business School Publishing, 2014, https://www.amazon.com/Conscious-Capitalism-New-Preface-Authors/dp/1625271751.

CHAPTER 6
BREAKING THE PARADOXES
TO INNOVATE FOR GOOD

Teresa Spangler

Context – On Breaking the Paradoxes

At the time of my writing this, the world is in the midst of unprecedented triple crises. The COVID-19 pandemic is wreaking havoc on healthcare and on the personal lives of people globally. The economic impacts of this pandemic are crippling nations, small towns, and people all over the world. And to top it off we are experiencing incredible social unrest – protests for *Black Lives Matter* are taking shape all around the world, with the goal of peaceful protests for change – but they've been hijacked by anarchists of varied profiles... individual crusaders, terrorists acting solo, antagonists of the left and the right wings... so many different factions creating chaos. All of this to say, change is happening at paces unimaginable and 'INNOVATION for Good' – of all types, centered on human, economic, and environmental impacts – is a dire necessity.

The world faces many great challenges. For example, the World Economic Forum reports that "by 2050, global food systems will need to sustainably and nutritiously feed more than nine billion people while providing economic opportunities in both rural and urban communities. Yet our food systems are falling far short of these goals. A systemic transformation is needed at an unprecedented *speed and scale*."[1]

Speed and scale, these days, are the operative words prioritized in innovation investments. When and how are the big questions that investors and stakeholders primarily ask. Of course these are important questions. Breaking the cycle of 'profit first' is not an easy shift for capitalist societies. *Social Entrepreneurism*, *Social Innovation Organizations*, and *Non-Governmental Organizations* are charting courses toward innovating in new and socially impactful ways, but they need the support, collaborative partnership, and help from investors and from the public and private sectors.

The world of business has been groomed for years to drive everything fast, faster, and fastest – fail-fast, rapid prototype, accelerated stage gates, hire-slow-fire-fast, rapid returns... and so on. Measured return on investments drives innovation decision-making from new cure-all drugs to the closet full of patents that sit in the coffers of giant industry leaders never making it out into the commercial world, even though these may be game-changing, lifesaving, humanity-improving innovations.

This chapter looks at examples of how to shift from 'profit first' to 'ethics and innovation for good and safety first'. If you build it safely, ethically, and build it to serve humanity, improve the environment, and support socially good causes, the profits will come. But investors and stakeholders need to understand the WHYs – why *safety*, *ethics*, and *serving* are so important. How are we innovators sharing these three critical priorities in the stories we build to gain buy-in on new ideas? So often, safety and ethics are afterthoughts. "If we do not critically and systematically assess our technologies in terms of the values they support and embody, people with perhaps less noble intentions may insert their views on sustainability, safety and security, health and well-being, privacy and accountability."[2]

In the textbook **Responsible Innovation: Ethics and Risks of New Technologies**, cited are case study examples of how conflicting values can open up new opportunities to innovate responsibly. As a learning method, the case study opens up our minds to the point of view of moral foundations as an opportunity: "Moral dilemmas can help stimulate creativity and innovation, and innovative design may help us to overcome problems of moral overload."[3]

> **In the case study excerpt below:** "Smart meters and conflicting values as an opportunity to innovate", the case study points to an example of smart meter design.
>
> *The smart meter 3.0, which is what we are ideally looking for, is designed to accommodate both of the functional requirements in order to make energy use more efficient, while also protecting personal data. It gives us privacy and sustainability. In this respect, innovation in smart metering is exactly this: the reconciliation of a range of values, or moral requirements, in one smart design, some of which were actually in conflict before.*

Similarly, if we would like to benefit from RFID technology (enabling to automatically identify and track tags attached to objects) in retail, but fear situations in which we might be tracked throughout the shopping mall, it has been suggested we can have it both ways. A so-called 'clipped chip' in the form of a price tag with clear indentations would allow customers to tear off a piece of the label, thereby shortening the antenna in the label so as to limit the range in which the label can transmit data.

Clarity of Values-Based Purpose

In the case above, there is clear purpose-driven innovation. Study after study has shown clarity of purpose is key to engaging people in new ideas.

A Kin&Co survey conducted by Populus points out that "Not embedding purpose properly also alienates customers, because in this age of transparency employee problems leak out online, and into the press. Over a third of employees surveyed (34%) said they'd consider writing a negative review online." One example cited is of "... the Etsy employee who started a petition against the company's leaders for not living their purpose and values, which was signed by thousands of employees and then went viral." The conclusion was thus that...

Having a purpose and not living it will actually hurt your business more than not having one at all.[4]

There is a hunger for more transparency, having our work be meaningful, and knowledge that ethics and privacy are forethoughts, not afterthoughts. It's good for business, and certainly will drive better profits in the long run.

Breaking the 'Fast Profit' Addiction and Adapting Innovation for Social Benefits – Seeking Purpose

> *Without tradition, art is a flock of sheep without a shepherd. Without innovation, it is a corpse.*
> **Winston Churchill[5]**

What if we asked the BIG 'What if?' What if we were more focused on the benefits of our innovations to humans, the environment, and society – making these priorities over profits first? Can it be proven that if you build it, the profits will come?

The United Nations: Sustainable Development Goals (SDGs)

The chapter *Foundations of Moral Innovation* (Chapter 3 – page 67) mentioned the 'triple bottom line' that socially conscious companies focus on serving – People / Planet / Profit... the social, environmental, and financial aspects of an organization's impact. In 2015 the United Nations cast a vision (and put actions to their words) to build a better world for all people by 2030. Engaging a world of collaborators is key to the success of these 17 Development Goals.

*"**The 17 Sustainable Development Goals (SDGs)** are the world's best plan to build a better world for people and our planet by 2030. Adopted by all United Nations Member States in 2015, the SDGs are a call for action by all countries – poor, rich and middle-income – to promote prosperity while protecting the environment. They recognize that ending poverty must go hand-in-hand with strategies that build economic growth and address a range of social needs including education, health, equality, and job opportunities, while tackling climate change and working to preserve our ocean and forests."[6]*

The *Division for Sustainable Development Goals* (DSDG)[7] within the United Nations *Department of Economic and Social Affairs* (UNDESA)[8] provides substantive support and capacity-building for these SDGs and their related thematic issues.

To say the least, as we read these 17 audaciously massive and impactful goals, the goals feel incredibly lofty; the actions to innovate solutions for three of the goals, much less 17 of them, feels nearly unachievable (in our fast prototyping, rapid release, ROI-focused, capitalistic mind-sets) and CFOs around the world sense that acting on these in any way may weigh heavily on profits. Yet many companies are collaborating to drive solutions to these goals. The United Nations built a values-based and purpose-driven platform to participate in solving these world challenges. They provide guidelines, research, information on other collaborators, tools, data, and so much support to help those that choose to participate. And participating they are! Noted from a press release in July 2019: "**28 companies with combined market cap of $1.3 trillion step up to new level of climate ambition.** Ahead of the UN Climate Action Summit, companies commit to set 1.5°C climate targets aligned with a net-zero future, challenging governments to match their ambition".[9]

Here are a few of the participating companies from this release: AstraZeneca, Banka BioLoo, BT, Dalmia Cement Ltd., Eco-Steel Africa Ltd., Enel, Hewlett Packard Enterprise, Iberdrola, KLP, Levi Strauss & Co., Royal DSM, SAP, Signify, Singtel, Telefonica, Telia, Unilever, Vodafone Group PLC, and Zurich Insurance, amongst others. The release goes on to note that this collectively represents over one million employees from 17 sectors and more than 16 countries.

It seems that the United Nations has created an intensely collaborative framework that offers a moral ground to innovate. It's just one example, and as complex as these goals are, the framework is simple... build a mission-driven platform, engage thought-leaders around the world, set up metrics and measures for success, provide as much data as possible, offer support when and where needed, and provide as many tools as possible to encourage collaboration amongst them.

ESG – A Moral Compass

Social investors are a group growing in popularity and size. These investors focus their investments and their portfolios on corporations around the world with metric-driven processes to ensure they are building sustainable and responsible companies – a practice known as environmental, social and corporate governance, or ESG[10].

An example of such an organization is Philips Corporation, which has made a commitment to ESG and thus to ethics over profits. In the article, "Good business: Why placing ethics over profits pays off", they share "When companies work ethically, they will naturally outpace competition. Why? Simply because customers, as we've discovered, will see them as a trusted partner, not only for what they do, but how it is delivered. Commitment from management is a key factor to effectively deal with these situations."[11]

In *Stanford Social Innovation Review*, authors Chris Fabian and Robert Fabricant write, "An ethical framework – 'a way of structuring your deliberation about ethical questions' – can help to bridge disparate worlds and discourses and help them work well together."[12] Their article further notes that, "Ethical questions might include: 'Is this platform / product actually providing a social good?' or 'Am I harming / including the user in the creation of this new solution?' or even 'Do I have a right to be taking claim of this space at all?'"[12] Such a strong ethical framework can help innovators to plan for 'value-based collaborations'. Establishing such a framework within your innovation practice also provides a process whereby collaborators can monitor the work, and consistently ensure that ethics are intact. Moreover, planning for positive outcomes and managing to an ethical framework gives customers, buyers, stakeholders, users, and investors some comfort that the 'net new disruptive innovations' will be safe for all, which will result in strong profits and longevity in due time.

Very importantly, this article also points out that while ethics may involve subjectivity, nevertheless "an ethical framework can bridge the worlds of startup technology companies and international development to strengthen cross-sector innovation in the social sector."[12]

Fabian and Fabricant outline a 4-model framework in this article:[12]

- *Innovation is humanistic: solving big problems through human ingenuity, imagination, and entrepreneurialism that can come from anywhere.*

- *Innovation is non-hierarchical: drawing ideas from many different sources and incubating small, agile teams to test and iterate on them with user feedback.*

- *Innovation is participatory: designing with (not for) real people.*

- *Innovation is sustainable: building skills even if most individual endeavors will ultimately fail in their societal goals.*

Harvesting the Human Imagination
– And Three Additional Considerations

Critical to the world's innovation effort is harvesting the Human Imagination!
Patrick Reasonover – writer and producer of
They Say It Can't Be Done

Incorporating any of the above four models provides the basis for forethought and planning. There may be additional considerations accompanying the above framework to drive even better outcomes yet – especially for those with big audacious visions of disruptive innovation. But often there are unexpected barriers. So how can one plan for the unexpected? There is a documentary film that explores some of these barriers, and four companies working to overcome them.

They Say It Can't Be Done, written and produced by Patrick Reasonover, is an excellent documentary exploring how innovation can solve some of the world's largest problems. The film tracks four companies on the cutting edge of technological solutions that could promote animal welfare, solve hunger, eliminate organ wait lists, and reduce atmospheric carbon. The film explores often unexpected challenges and barriers that are potentially keeping these companies from realizing success. They each share steps and strategies on how to break through the 'concrete walls'.[13]

The compelling theme from these companies is ***innovation for good*** – innovation with a moral foundation to improve humanity. One of the first questions typically asked by stakeholders is "When will these companies or their new innovations become profitable?" Here's the BIG 'What if' question. **What if** we changed this question to, **"What will it take to make this successful, and how can we help you get there faster?"** These are fairly typical questions. But what about roadblocks potentially challenging even the most knowledgeable and experienced teams and proven technologies? I recently spoke with **Patrick Reasonover** about his mission and the documentary. Reasonover shares, "Faced with similar challenges to the companies in the documentary, I felt if more people understood barriers, the world would see more successful outcomes that could save people, improve human conditions, and the environment." Reasonover went on to share four themes that would greatly help disruptors in their innovation practices.

These four themes are summarized as follows:

1. One of the most important points he made in our discussion was to engage regulators and government agencies – collaborating with them very early on in the process and all along your path. Help them to understand; listen and take in their input.

2. Institute what Reasonover calls an 'Ambassador of Imagination'. We need more imagination in the world and in our own world. It's too easy to get boxed into an innovation framework and forget to take the blinders off in order to think and create big things!

3. Optimism is sorely needed in the world and especially for innovators. Getting new things out the door is daunting. Infuse your efforts with doses of optimism grounded in reality.

4. <u>CELEBRATE</u>... hitting milestones should be celebrated along the way. It's a long road, and all too often we get push back from doubters, investors wanting faster outcomes, governing approval agencies, and so on. Celebrate and move forward!

These four practices create a culture that encourages and celebrates imagination, innovation, success, and all the collaborators helping you get there. And involving agencies early on in the process helps them to understand that you are taking safety and ethics seriously. Take for example 3D-printed organs for those needing transplants. There is so much at stake. Stepping through the approval process to prove it out on less risky organs – for example, 3D printed ears – helps to chart the course for other organs as the technologies and the discovery of new methods continues to develop.

The article "On The Road To 3-D Printed Organs" in *TheScientist* reports, "There are a number of companies who are attempting to do things like 3-D print ears, and researchers have already reported transplanting 3-D printed ears onto children who had birth defects that left their ears underdeveloped, notes Robby Bowles, a bioengineer at the University of Utah. The ear transplants are, he says, 'kind of the first proof of concept of 3-D printing for medicine.'"[14, 15]

Ethics First

All in all, there is much evidence pointing to success, longevity, scale, and profits when building a framework that places ethics, safety, values, and purpose as planned practices in any innovation effort.

These practices do not have to slow the process of innovation in the least. On the contrary... they will often speed up the effort, as in the example of engaging regulators as collaborators early on in your efforts. Engaging imagination and optimism are sorely needed, and keeps teams engaged and enthused. And.. leveraging one of Stanford's four models could save a great deal of pain by monitoring outcomes all along your development stage gates. It all just makes good and safe business sense!

End Notes

---

1   World Economic Forum, "Innovation with a Purpose: The role of technology innovation in accelerating food systems transformation", 23 January 2018, https://fr.weforum.org/reports/innovation-with-a-purpose-the-role-of-technology-innovation-in-accelerating-food-systems-transformation.

2   Responsible Innovation: Ethics and Risks of New Technologies, Joost Groot Kormelink, TU Delft Open, 2019, https://open.umn.edu/opentextbooks/textbooks/responsible-innovation-ethics-safety-and-technology.

3   Responsible Innovation: Ethics and Risks of New Technologies, page 32.

4   "Comment: Why purpose matters and four steps companies can take to get it right", Rosie Warin, 14 February 2018, Ethical Corporation Magazine, Reuters Events – Sustainable Business, https://www.ethicalcorp.com/comment-why-purpose-matters-and-four-steps-companies-can-take-get-it-right.

5   "Churchill Art Blooms in London", Allen Packwood, Education – Pentland Churchill Design Competition, Finest Hour 160, Autumn 2013, p. 54, https://winstonchurchill.org/publications/finest-hour/finest-hour-160/education-pentland-churchill-design-competition/.

6   "Transforming Our World: The 2030 Agenda for Sustainable Development", A/RES/70/1, United Nations, New York, September 2015, https://sustainabledevelopment.un.org/post2015/transformingourworld/publication.

7   United Nations Division for Sustainable Development Goals (DSDG), https://sdgs.un.org/about.

8   United Nations Department of Economic and Social Affairs (UNDESA), https://www.un.org/development/desa/en/.

9   "28 companies with combined market cap of $1.3 trillion step up to new level of climate ambition", Press Release, UN Sustainable Development Goals, New York, July 2019, https://www.un.org/sustainabledevelopment/blog/2019/07/un-global-compact-pr/.

10 Wikipedia entry on Environmental, Social, and Corporate Governance, https://en.wikipedia.org/wiki/Environmental,_social_and_corporate_governance.

11 "Good business: Why placing ethics over profits pays off", Roy Jakobs, Innovation Matters Blog, Philips Corporation, https://www.philips.com/a-w/about/news/archive/blogs/innovation-matters/good-business-why-placing-ethics-over-profits-pays-off.html.

[12] "The Ethics of Innovation", Chris Fabian, Robert Fabricant, *Stanford Social Innovation Review – Technology & Design*, 05 August 2014, https://ssir.org/articles/entry/the_ethics_of_innovation#.

[13] They Say It Can't Be Done, Patrick Reasonover, https://www.crowdcast.io/theysayitcantbedone.

[14] "On the Road to 3-D Printed Organs", Emma Yasinski, *TheScientist*, 26 February 2020, https://www.the-scientist.com/news-opinion/on-the-road-to-3-d-printed-organs-67187.

[15] "In Vitro Regeneration of Patient-specific Ear-shaped Cartilage and Its First Clinical Application for Auricular Reconstruction", Guangdong Zhou, Haiyue Jiang, Zongqi Yin, Yu Liu, Qingguo Zhang, Chen Zhang, Bo Pan, Jiayu Zhou, Xu Zhou, Hengyun Sun, Dan Li, Aijuan He, Zhiyong Zhang, Wenjie Zhang, Wei Liu, Yilin Cao, *EBioMedicine*, Volume 28, p. 287-302, 01 February 2018, The Lancet, https://www.sciencedirect.com/science/article/pii/S2352396418300161.

CHAPTER 7

ORGANIZATIONAL VALUES – AN ESSENTIAL TOOL FOR CREATING A CULTURE OF INNOVATION

Bryan W. Mattimore

Not long after 9/11, the Con Edison company contacted me about delivering a keynote speech on creativity and innovation for their NYC-based middle managers and senior executives. You may know that during 9/11, Con Ed employees went to heroic lengths to restore power in record time to businesses and residents of lower Manhattan.

I think the Con Ed executives were seeing my talk, which was part of a day-long training and employee enrichment program, as a kind of reward for all the hard work their employees had done after the attack on the Twin Towers, as well as a way to send the message that innovation was – and would continue to be – an important organizational value.

I was both deeply honored and slightly embarrassed by their invitation. They had been on the front lines fighting terrorism, and I had been sitting at home in Connecticut watching TV and drinking diet soda. To earn the right to address them, I felt I needed a way – even if it was relatively insignificant – to empathize with what they had been through.

And so I asked a member of the Con Edison leadership team if I could spend a day in the field with their employees: service technicians, power plant managers, emergency response teams, etc. To my surprise, they agreed, and gave me virtually unlimited access.

On the appointed day, after signing the necessary waivers, I donned a Con Edison hard hat and was off. I rode the trucks, toured the power plants, even crawled through the maze of steam heating pipes in Rockefeller Center looking for leaks. It was an extraordinary experience at so many levels, including being a lot of fun. What I hadn't anticipated was that it would change forever how I viewed my work as an innovation consultant.

For each of the more than a dozen Con Ed employees I 'worked with' that day, I asked two simple questions:

1. "What's something you would change at work?" (thank you, Peter Drucker, for this question), and

2. "In all your years working at Con Ed, what are you most proud of?"

Question number one gave me great insight into what was and wasn't working 'on the front lines' that I was able to incorporate into my keynote. But It was question number two that provided me with my Eureka, life changing moment.

Every employee I asked the 'most proud of' question, without exception, said that it was an idea they came up with, and that the company subsequently implemented, they were most proud of. And these were not necessarily big ideas. It could have been a simple cost cutting recommendation, a suggestion to make service calls more efficient, or a novel approach to managing the power grid to better accommodate energy spikes on hot summer days.

Mo, a 25-year Con Ed veteran, and my companion inspecting the Rockefeller Center steam pipe leaks, told me that it was his idea to have the company tie in the workers' cell phones with customer service, so they could be connected at all times with customer requests, no matter where they were on the job site.

It became obvious to me that day that everyone in an organization not only has the potential, but as importantly, the need to contribute new ideas to help their company grow and prosper.

In the years since that day, my belief in creating an environment where all employees are encouraged to make meaningful creative contributions to their organization has only strengthened. Being able to contribute new ideas is critical to an employee's sense of self… and ultimately self-worth. It is both wasteful – and frankly unkind – to allow an employee's creative potential to go unrealized.

From an organizational perspective, it may well be that the most under-leveraged organizational asset is the creativity of its employees. How then can organizational leaders create organizational structures that foster and exploit this unrealized creative potential so important to not only the organization – but to the employees as well?

I can't think of a single Fortune 500 company that my innovation agency has worked with in the past three years, where their leadership didn't recognize that in these times of accelerated change, unanticipated disruptions (including of course the COVID-19 pandemic of 2020), and increasingly-fierce domestic and global competition, that 'innovating the future' wasn't critical. They recognize that creating innovation structures that ensure continuous innovation, accomplished with great speed and agility, is now a prerequisite to their organization's very survival.

And so, to their credit, these companies have pioneered new models for innovation. Importantly, these new models go way beyond the closer-in, 'business-as-usual' creation of line extensions and product service tweaks. No, specially-designated innovation teams are now:

— pioneering white space opportunities, often between divisions, that are innovating entirely new product or service platforms;

— developing open innovation programs to incubate and/or joint venture with start-ups;

— establishing their own venture funds to promote and profit by investing in new ventures in associated industries;

— partnering with other companies to invent and offer products and services they would or could not offer on their own, and certainly not with the same speed that the partnership allows;

— teaming with a wide variety of trend agencies, technology research services, and consumer research firms to inform the invention – or acquisition – of synergistic, and on-trend new business opportunities.

These new innovation models are revolutionizing how innovation is done today.

Unfortunately, these innovation models do not involve the entire organization. The majority of the organization's employees typically don't work in strategy, marketing, or product development, and therefore don't have the opportunity to make nearly as many, if any, new idea contributions to the organization. One can only imagine the loss in creative productivity, not to mention employee satisfaction, by not having a process and a culture that encourages creative contributions from everyone.

That's not to say that companies haven't tried, and aren't continuing to try, to encourage idea submissions from all employees in traditionally less-than 'idea-driven' departments. Suggestion box programs are the best known of these initiatives. However, with few exceptions (Toyota, Dart Industries, Frito-Lay, etc.) suggestion box programs have been dismal failures. A lack of follow-up and development of submitted ideas, along with ill-conceived reward programs, have been the two main reasons for their failure.

Electronic 'suggestion box' platforms from Spigit, Brightidea, Ezassi, Planbox, and others have fared better, but can also suffer from a lack of internal support and effective follow-through, much like traditional suggestion box programs. 'Hackathons' and Shark Tank-type competitions have on occasion succeeded, but these are usually one-time events, and don't necessarily promote a culture change that continuously encourages the sharing of new ideas from all employees.

What about leading more and different kinds of ideation sessions with employees from across the organization? Traditionally, ideation sessions are used to generate:

— new growth strategies;

— new product and service ideas;

— product positioning and development concepts;

— new sales strategies; and

— advertising, promotion, and social media ideas;

... and as such, rarely involve employees outside these specialized areas of expertise.

Fortunately, this narrow focus on running only new product, marketing, strategy or advertising ideation sessions is also changing. My innovation agency, for instance, has been tasked with designing and facilitating a wide range of non-traditional ideation sessions – both as stand-alone projects, but also as part of larger, organizational-wide Total Innovation Enterprise consulting initiatives.

These sessions include creating innovative ideas, processes, and programs to:

- improve customer experience and loyalty;
- reinvent logistics and supply chain methodologies;
- recruit and retain talent;
- develop innovative sales strategies;
- communicate more effectively both internally and externally;
- reduce costs organization-wide;
- develop cross-divisional process initiatives to improve efficiency while also reducing time to market;
- more effectively integrate a new acquisition;
- improve the effectiveness of training programs;
- identify and promote potential strategic contributions from finance and accounting;
- increase manufacturing output and plant safety;
- improve sustainability.

And this is a promising trend. But even though these creative applications of ideation processes frequently lead to successful outcomes, they are still one-shots. They generate solutions for the specific identified challenges, but fall short of true culture change, again in part, because they involve only a small percentage of the entire organization's workforce, and they are not practiced continuously.

So, what's the answer? What will help create a culture of creativity and innovation where all employees feel empowered to continuously generate new ideas to benefit the organization… and in the process meet their own, inherent need for personal growth and self-actualization? One answer we've discovered is to re-focus the organization on their vision, mission, and values, but particularly their values.

A vision, most readers will know, is the 'reason for being' of an organization. In succinct and simple language, it makes clear how the organization aspires to serve its constituents while making the world a better place. Disney's, "To Make People Happy," or Charles Schwab's, "Helping Investors Help Themselves," are two good examples.

If the vision represents the 'why' of an organization, the mission makes clear the 'how' – specifically, how the organization is going to achieve the vision. Typically, a mission includes a 3 - 5 year future view of the organization. Here's Toyota's mission:

> *Toyota will lead the way to the future of mobility, enriching lives around the world with the safest and most responsible ways of moving people. Through our commitment to quality, constant innovation and respect for the planet, we aim to exceed expectations and be rewarded with a smile. We will meet challenge goals by engaging the talent and passion of people, who believe there is always a better way.*

Creating, and communicating the vision and mission, is the job of senior leadership.

Values, on the other hand, are and should be more democratic: they are what support and inform the vision and mission, and shape the culture. And because they represent what the organization 'values' – its essential principles and beliefs – they also guide and model behavior of every employee at every level of the organization. Two of the most important 'values' of values are the following. First, they help employees in the decision-making process, both in determining what to do, and equally as important, what NOT to do. Second, if supported and continually re-affirmed by the organization's leadership, they can also inspire and encourage daily creative contributions.

Zappos, the legendary online shoe and fashion retailer was at one point facing bankruptcy. According to CEO Tony Hsieh, it wasn't until they crystallized their own vision, mission, and values – but especially their values – that the company turned around and ultimately sold to Amazon in November 2009 for $1.2 billion. Interestingly, creating and then settling on their ten values was a year-long process that involved everyone in the organization.

Zappos's ten values are:

1. Deliver WOW through service.

2. Embrace and drive change.

3. Be adventurous, creative, and open-minded.

4. Pursue growth and learning.

5. Build open and honest relationships with communication.

6. Build a positive team and family spirit.

7. Do more with less.

8. Be passionate and determined.

9. Be humble. And...

10. Create fun and a little weirdness.

I have yet to find a medium or large size organization without at least one value that doesn't champion the importance of creative thinking, innovation, or growth. In Zappos' case, at least three of their values implicitly or explicitly focus on the importance of being creative: numbers 2, 3, and 10.

Since values that stress creative organization-wide contributions are already being championed by senior leadership, they create an opportunity – and tacit approval – for internal change agents to create more and better organizational initiatives, programs, and processes that encourage 'everyday' employee creativity.

Pragmatically speaking, what might some of these programs and processes be? How can values, specifically, be used to encourage ongoing creative contributions from all employees? A critical first step of course is to determine where the organization is in relation to its own values creation and acceptance.

If the organization's values have not yet been created, or as importantly, not continually championed in an inspirational and actionable way, then it may be time to either: a) create new values, or b) re-energize the current ones.

When my innovation agency leads vision, mission, and values creation projects for a client, it's a given that vision and mission are the purview of the organization's leadership. But in creating the organization's values, we involve every employee in the process. Here's how:

1. All employees are asked to submit their ideas for the values.

2. A values committee made up of organization representatives from all levels and all departments reviews and themes the often literally thousands of 'values' submissions.

3. This committee then decides on both the themes, and the specific language they would like to recommend to the organization's leadership committee and/or board.

4. The values are agreed upon by both the values committee and the organization's leadership. The number of values typically ranges from 5 to 10.

5. The final values are then shared with the entire organization.

This is only the first of many steps, however, to use the values as a vehicle for encouraging the suggestion, development, and launch of new ideas.

After the values have been agreed upon and announced, we lead (or train internal facilitators to lead), 3-hour 'values implementation' workshops with all employees. In these workshops, each employee learns and applies a variety of ideation techniques that help them to reimagine their day-to-day jobs in ways that are informed and inspired by the organization's stated values. These imaginative, job reinvention techniques include customer wishing, job mind-mapping, and a-day-in-the-life.

These values implementation workshops are a critical step to creating an organization-wide culture of innovation for several reasons:

1. They clearly send the message that having organizational values is NOT so that a pretty plaque can be hung on the wall with some inspirational words on it; rather, they are intended to inspire and direct every aspect of an employee's work.

2. They expose all employees to a variety of personal team ideation techniques they can use in all aspects of their jobs to generate new ideas.

3. Since one of the values is invariably about being creative, they send the message that being creative in their day-to-day jobs is critically important.

4. They set the stage for ongoing, organization-wide values popularization and activation programs.

What are some examples of these popularization and activation programs, especially as they might relate to using values to inspire a 'culture of innovation?' Here are two.

One of our clients creates 'values newsletters' for all their employees that highlight a different organizational value each month. So, for instance, one of their seven organizational values is, "Be a Pioneer."

The values newsletter featuring the "Be a Pioneer" value encourages employees to exhibit behaviors that reflect such words as "introduce, launch, initiate, spearhead, found, originate, create, blaze a trail, and make the first move." The newsletter also features reviews of books and TED talks that contain principles and case studies of 'pioneering behavior.' And finally, organization leaders are encouraged to begin all their team meetings with a short discussion of what it means to "Be a Pioneer." The continuing focus on values – month in and month out – is critical for evolving the organizational culture to a more innovative one.

The second technique we use to help institutionalize the value of creativity we call The Whiteboard Technique. It is a very simple technique, and it can be done either virtually or at an organization's offices. In a physical office setting, the manager places a whiteboard in a public location and records a challenge for which she wants new ideas. Co-workers are then encouraged to add ideas for a pre-determined length of time – usually seven to ten days. As employees add ideas each day, the number of ideas grows dramatically, which can inspire ideas that both build on existing ideas, as well as spark entirely new ones. After the allotted time, the manager who posted the creative challenge selects the most promising ideas for future development and/or implementation. Then another creative challenge is posted. Unlike a suggestion box program, the whiteboard technique can be used to elicit ideas for a wide range of very specific challenges, while at the same time encouraging build-on ideas.

There's a popular notion in creative problem-solving circles: don't try to solve a challenge by attacking it head-on... rather approach it by 'thinking to the side.' Creating a culture of innovation by using the organization's values as a vehicle for continually reminding all employees about both the importance of – and the organization's receptivity to – new ideas, is a wonderful 'thinking to the side' strategy. And it's one that every employee, as they begin to realize their own creative potential, should thank you for.

CHAPTER 8

INNOVATION HAS A
MUCH BIGGER ROLE TO PLAY

Mike Pinder

Innovation and Human Progress

Innovation has undoubtedly been a significant driver of human progress, in truly remarkable ways. From the simple wheel, to the printing press, steam power, antibiotics, electricity, and the transistor, to name just a few. If you have not yet seen it, the film *2001: A Space Odyssey* does a wonderful job of chronicling our past and future ascension as we progress through waves of technological change.[1]

The practice of innovation is uniquely-positioned to bring about drastic changes in the world, with potential for tremendous positive impact across societies, economies, and entire ecosystems. What hinders this impact? What needs to change now for innovation to flourish in this space? How do people and the environment benefit simultaneously whilst addressing the most serious global challenges we face? This chapter aims to highlight and give direction to these pressing issues and challenges surrounding innovation today.

Innovation and Institutions

The act of innovating involves new creative thinking applied to problem solving in novel ways, leading to commercial profit and ideally some kind of societal improvement at large, and has been in this sequence for a long time. Innovation has mostly been a good thing for us, by driving unrivalled economic prosperity, increased social wellbeing and mobility, whilst creating vastly prosperous nations. Key underlying and supporting institutions have been carefully designed and developed over many decades to ensure innovation (and new economic growth) can thrive repeatedly and systematically in a competitive marketplace. As a result, we enjoy longer, healthier lives with better prospects than prior generations.

Innovation and Continuous Growth

So how did innovation help to achieve these progressive feats? The answer lies in purposefully intertwining the need for innovation with the concept of growth. In particular, economic growth; defined as an increase in the amount of goods and services produced per head of the population over a period of time. Or put another way, when output rises, job opportunities are created which permit a rise in income and mobility.[2]

In order to achieve economic growth, innovation provides the systematic means and process to enable the development and application of new ideas and technologies, used to increase the creation of new goods and services that result in more efficient production outputs. Innovation also increases the total output amount possible (given our resource constraints) by making us more productive, ultimately stimulating wages and further business profitability. More productivity and profitability mean the economy grows, resulting in greater reinvestments and more jobs to go around. This sounds great. Who would not want this?

The challenge is this: in order to keep perpetual growth happening, the same finite inputs and resources must continually generate greater and greater outputs to sustain itself over a given time. This is challenging to say the least, if not impossible to achieve.

Continuous economic growth is all well and good at the individualistic level, but there are serious positive *and* negative consequences, as we are all too well aware. One simply cannot keep doing the same thing and expect different results, as the saying goes (incidentally a commonly-cited definition of insanity). Adam Smith's ideas for fundamental economics – established back in 1759 – describe the *invisible hand* automatically leading us to desirable benefits for all, simply by leaving free markets and growth to regulate themselves.[3] Driven by self-interest, this concept has clearly not led to universal social and environmental utopia as was predicted several hundred years ago. It is arguably quite the opposite in modern times.[4]

The need and pursuit of perpetual economic growth creates *the* market driven alibi to rally innovation into action. In so doing, influencing new policy, private investment, R&D, public spending, and so forth. Innovation provides one of the most effect mechanisms we have of continually achieving sustained (not sustainable) economic growth. It is tightly bound into our collective beliefs, culture, and logic around the organization of business, health, and education.[5] Media outlets and politicians echo similar sentiments with quantitative econometrics to track progress at the country level using gross domestic product (GDP), inflation, unemployment, exchange rates, consumer spending, plus many other measures. This type of metric fails at taking into account crucial elements such as inequality issues, levels of happiness and joy, entrepreneurial agency, social mobility, and environmental issues of a qualitative nature. Standard progress metrics provide a quantitative snapshot of economic progress and growth, but little else. With innovation being focused on people with unmet needs and problems (often at an emotional level), it is easy to see how this kind of growth progress tracking is disconnected from everyday human experience.

Innovation, People, and the Wider World

Innovation is typically triggered by inquisitive visionaries who purposefully imagine a more desirable future state rather than to just bring new growth to economies. They are driven by challenging the status quo with novel ideas to test with potentially profitable business ecosystems to validate. New concepts and new business models act as two sides of the same coin, and have the power to deliver different ways of achieving our jobs to be done, with positive and/or negative intended and/or unintended consequences.

The documentary *Extinction: The Facts*[6] by Sir David Attenborough outlined the ways in which human development under the guise of economic growth has continued to negatively influence our planet. On climate alone, the year 2020 (the year of its publication) was already the hottest year in recorded history, without any El Niño or solar storm event to be accountable for that fact.

We do not need yet another documentary to point out what we are patently aware of. There are serious consequences for all of us if we continue to exist in an unsustainable way with perpetual economic growth at the heart of things as the dominant paradigm. Climate change, loss of biodiversity, population increase, and global pandemics are just a glimpse at the tip of the melting iceberg in front of all of us.

Innovation and Creative Destruction

A term already exists describing the relentless and continuous need for economic growth by innovating, and the inevitable undesirable and unforeseen consequences. Coined *Creative Destruction* back in the early 20th century, it states that innovation and growth are dependent upon dismantling long-standing practices in order to make way for new configurations. You have to destroy something as you make way for something new. Destroying the old as a result of implementing something new, through improved methods in the act of production.[7] A contemporary example of this is Netflix, who introduced an entirely different business model that eventually overthrew the disc rental business and all the infrastructure, dependent industries, intellectual property, jobs, and livelihoods that went with it. Other examples include airplanes replacing rail (and more recently vice-versa), telephones and fax machines replacing delivered mail, and Internet shopping replacing physical retail spaces. Long standing *best practices*, procedures, products, and services get replaced by new disruptive ideas and technologies, oftentimes with inferior features offering more convenience and performance for the same or cheaper costs than previously incurred.[8]

Creative destruction begins to explain the detrimental impact of uncontrolled and unregulated human activity purely for the sake of economic growth alone – tied to the imperative for new shareholder value and short-term profits. This thinking and logic results in negative unanticipated or unintended environmental and social consequences, with impacts felt broadly. For instance, the COVID-19 pandemic of 2020 wrought untold economic global turmoil, and was a sobering reminder of the consequences of encroaching too far into nature's habitat in pursuit of new economic growth.

Interestingly and conversely, the concept of creative destruction offers a future glimpse of hope for us at the species level, because it is through the creative destruction process that we can begin to dismantle old ways of achieving our essential *jobs to be done*.[9] If used appropriately, we can use innovation to explore better ways to serve our needs whilst reducing negative environmental, ecological, and social consequences for us all.

Innovation has continually demonstrated the potential to destroy us environmentally, socially, *and* economically; or enable us to thrive sustainably. It is our collective choice. If used in the right collective way, innovation has the power to continuously revolutionize and reform our economic structures and institutions from within, destroying the old ways of governing and managing ourselves, whilst replacing them with new and better ways.

For the most part of our development, the economic element of the equation has been far less of a casualty in comparison to the state of our global environment and supporting ecosystems. Ironically, those that our economies depend upon in the first place. Something is clearly not right, but we all know this. What to do about it, effectively, is the challenge.

New creative destruction reconfigurations are needed to fundamentally change the way we run our existing economic systems. By transforming them into more sustainable arrangements, we can actively design new and improved ways to address the global challenges facing us. This may sound like naïve, optimistic, wishful thinking, but there is also a strong business case behind it.

Corporate Experiences Innovating for Growth

Large corporate organizations – due to their power, size, and reach – are in a strong position to bring about drastic changes for the environment and society at large. Over the past 20 years, large corporates have been heavily focused on regaining competitive advantage over pesky disruptive start-ups by attempting to imitate and codify their ways of working to replicate in-house. Significant investments have been made in innovation methodologies like Design Thinking, Design Sprints, Lean Startup, Business Model Innovation, Agile, and growth hacking… in effect, how to do innovation at the same speed and cost. These methodologies and capabilities are deployed in various formats from short term Design Sprints to longer term innovation accelerators, supported by toolkits and playbooks for internal employees to follow. The intention is to drive new disruptive, radical, or architectural innovation from within corporate walls to grow equally valuable unicorn organizations – ultimately aiming to displace incumbents and ensure long-term survival. In reality, the number of unicorns emerging from corporate efforts whilst simultaneously solving global sustainability issues are few and far between. The point here is that the groundwork is being done, and seeds are being sown, to grow innovation capabilities to drive new sustainable change.

I have worked in innovation for over twelve years, guiding, training, and consulting over 2000+ smart people at small start-ups and global Fortune 500s, from executives and board members, down to project teams. We have so far codified the innovation process into easy-to-follow, step-by-step, replicable, and scalable methodologies using tools and frameworks such as Design Thinking, Lean Startup, Business Model Innovation, and Agile. Put together and used in the right way, they increase the speed and accuracy of knowing; and reduce uncertainty across the innovation process in order to drive iterative development of new products and services through to market and scaling.

We have thus far designed a somewhat universal approach to enable the efficient pursuit and exploitation of new ideas and business models to in turn enable economic growth, as prescribed by the requirements of our current industrial capitalism model and supporting institutions. This is important progress, but there is much more we need to do upgrade this approach to tackle the *wicked problems* we face together in the wider World.

Large firms are just coming to grips with iterative, customer-centric ways of working, whilst moving away from purely technological or inside out driven solutions, to problems that are not truly known to exist in the first place. Before these innovation methodologies become standard, universal practice, we need to roadmap ahead of time what needs to happen next for innovation.

Industrial Revolutions and Innovation Process

Over the past two decades, the means of production has been severely impacted by the democratizing effect of digitalization – and digital technology in general. More recently coined as *Industry 4.0*, it represents a blurring of the boundaries between the *technical*, *biological*, and *physical* spheres. It thus represents the general interconnectedness of traditionally separate specialized domains, where thinking and innovating can now happen seamlessly across them. This interconnectedness is crucial to triggering new waves of holistic innovation approaches that serve wider ecosystem needs, rather than for solving individual or market segment unmet needs and problems. The latter results in short-sighted, short-term shareholder value outcomes, and not much else. We can do better than this.

We are entering a new phase of possibilities where new frontiers of innovation are located at the cross-domain and discipline levels, spanning new ecosystems of stakeholder needs, internationally. The tools and methods we use for this new phase need to reflect this interconnectedness in order to solve bigger and broader challenges. For this to happen outside the myopic pursuit of economic growth alone, we must take the opportunity to evolve and develop the current innovation process more broadly to tackle entire ecosystems of unmet needs and problems, not just those of our customers and end-users. Innovation needs to level-up.

Design Thinking, Design Sprints, Lean Startup, Business Model Innovation, UX, Agile, and the like, simply must aim to do more than develop new products and services. We must evolve them to think bigger and more holistically to tackle the enormous collective challenges we face. I put it to the innovation community to take the innovation process as it is known today, and apply them more broadly to the challenges we face as a collective species. We can and must do a lot more with the tools of change that we have developed to create new value and growth by firmly embedding sustainability throughout the innovation process, as standard practice.

Innovation and Shifting Goal Posts

We have clear goalposts, as defined in 2015 by the UN Sustainable Development Goals[10], with the intention of achieving them each by 2030:

1	No Poverty	10	Reducing Inequality
2	Zero Hunger	11	Sustainable Cities & Communities
3	Good Health & Wellbeing	12	Responsible Consumption & Production
4	Quality Education	13	Climate Action
5	Gender Equality	14	Life Below Water
6	Clean Water & Sanitation	15	Life On Land
7	Affordable & Clean Energy	16	Peace, Justice, & Strong Institutions
8	Decent Work & Economic Growth	17	Partnerships for the Goals
9	Industry, Innovation, & Infrastructure		

However, each time we set ambitious targets, we spectacularly fail to meet them.[11] The recent Global Biodiversity Outlook study showed that we did not meet a single target related to the destruction of wildlife and life-sustaining ecosystems in the past decade.[12] These are vastly complex challenges, intrinsically linked to the nature of our economic system, and are not easy to change. But this does not mean we should not. We need innovation more than ever to challenge the status quo and come up with new ecosystem level concepts. Helping us to validate new ways of creating economic growth in sustainable ways that effectively solve the challenges we face.

How we do this is as yet not entirely known, but innovation certainly has the potential underlying process to propose new answers via new ideas and business models to get us there. As users, consumers, and citizens we all have that responsibility, but as innovation practitioners, we have the privilege of holding the keys that can unlock the doors to the right thinking. We must use innovation for the bigger issues.

A tremendous amount of change power also lies with those who 'do' innovation. Applying new business strategies, thinking, tools, and methods to solve new global challenges is at our fingertips. Innovation thought-leaders are the avant-garde change-makers of our sustainable futures, responsible for inspiring others away from apathetic indifference around the insurmountable changes needed ahead – at all levels of society.

We have long heard the phrase in Economics that supply equals demand. The power for change lies in each of us, in the small choices and decisions we make. If we change our modes, patterns, and levels of consumption, then value chains, businesses, policies, and governments will all be forced to change in response.

Innovation With Purpose

Organizations need leaders and innovators with a strong North Star purpose... those with a clear sense of where and how positive environmental and social contributions need to happen. This, coupled with a shared vision about creating mutual sustainable value, rather than just meeting the intense pressure of shareholder expectations and growing the economy for growth's sake.

Purpose-driven leaders within organizations need purpose-driven business strategies clearly linked to innovation strategy, and down to the team level.[13] This enables the execution of the overall mission and vision, underpinned by wider cultural values. This in turn ensures that innovation outcomes land somewhere in the organization, and have a chance to scale their impact. Leading organizations in this way helps to attract new talent who share these same beliefs and purposes – team members who are intrinsically motivated to create joint sustainable value for a bigger cause than themselves, rather than simply for the pay check.[14] More and more firms are making this trajectory shift whilst also remaining financially healthy and growing – as seen on lists like *Corporate Knights Global Sustainability Rankings* for example.[15]

Millennials and Gen-Zers are also applying pressure, by increasingly seeking employment at firms with a strong contribution compass to solve global challenges. This places further pressure on firms to adapt and change.

Sustainable innovation organizations need sustainable business models to support new disruptive, radical, and architectural innovation concepts, so that they create, deliver, and capture value for all stakeholders, without depleting natural, economic, and social capital.

We must disentangle and rewire our supporting institutions from strongly linking innovation with economic growth alone. Ideas have been suggested – like forcing firms to create public and private value; or collecting much broader data sets to allow investors to make sustainable choices on the stock markets.

At the organizational level, ensuring that employees always get to own a part of the firms they work for could be an option; or limiting investments to long term growth options, whilst rewarding those with dividends benefiting long-standing ecosystem shareholders. It has also been suggested to make firms take responsibility for the entirety of their value chains, as Nike has done; or implementing sustainability based environmental, social, governance models that can be fully auditable and accountable.[16]

Whilst these are potentially great ideas, suggestions, and concepts, we must use the innovation process, optimized for sustainability, to fully validate them in terms of desirability, viability, feasibility, *and* sustainability, as we bring them forward from the bottom-up and top-down, forcing new institutional change in its wake (reference Figure 4 below).

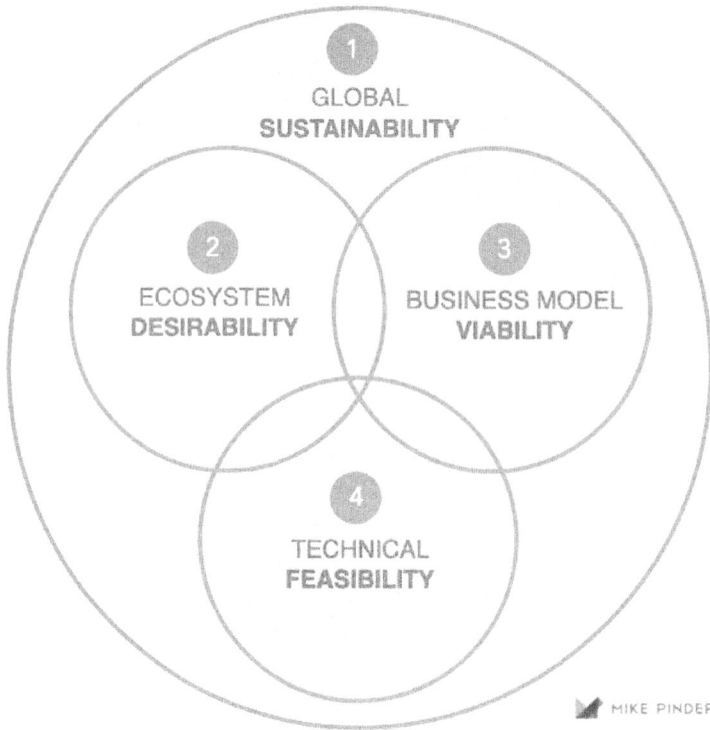

GLOBAL
SUSTAINABILITY

ECOSYSTEM
DESIRABILITY

BUSINESS MODEL
VIABILITY

TECHNICAL
FEASIBILITY

MIKE PINDER

Figure 4: Shifting the focus of innovation towards our collective global challenges.

Adapting Innovation to the Bigger Challenges

The good news is there are things happening on this frontier with the spread of the concepts such as *Circular Economy Innovation*.[17] I recently had the privilege of working with the World Economic Forum to design and develop a new innovation process, framework, playbook, and toolbox specifically aimed the national level, called Scale360°.[18] It is intended to foster local, regional, and national approaches to creating new sustainable circular economy innovation ecosystems to take advantage of the projected EUR 1.3 trillion market potential by 2030.[19] The aim is to think big from the outset, taking on and positively contributing to the UN's sustainable challenges. By looking at the broader stakeholder ecosystem levels, the aim is to drive new thinking to implement entirely new sustainable business models for validation, scaling, and impact.

The message here is that sustainable innovation is also big business. It has the potential to create substantial returns whilst solving the biggest global challenges we face. In order to do so, it needs to break the dominant economic logic and change its long-standing supporting institutions. If we begin to see climate change as the same critical priority and rally behind it whilst driving the right kind of constructive capitalism in support, then great change – impactful changes – can occur.

Innovating a Better Future

We need to move away from seeing the innovation process, tools, and methods as merely mimicking digital software development practices, transplanted onto and into large corporations, hoping that it will drive new growth a bit quicker. We need to build upon our knowledge decoded from how disruptive startups bootstrap their way to market scaling and growth. We need new practical tools, methods, and processes, like Scale360, that work to solve not only big global challenges across new ecosystems, but also put pressure on the institutions and governments that are configured to maintain the unsustainable status quo.

Critical global challenges require news ideas and new business models. And this is what innovation is designed to do and positioned to do. Just as we saw with the successful international response to the impact of CFCs on the ozone layer, or to the pandemic of 2020, if there is a big enough crisis, need, urge, or desire to solve big world challenges, then we will. To do so, we must challenge where we focus our problem-solving attention, and take global issues more seriously as critical innovation challenges to solve. At the same time, we must adapt what we have learned about organizational science over the past hundred years and update our thinking to solve the big global problems. If we do not act now, we will face severe, irreversible, run-away consequences in the near future. We already know this. It is time to really see what innovation can do for all our sakes.

End Notes

1 *2001: A Space Odyssey*, Stanley Kubrick, Arthur C. Clarke, Metro-Goldwyn-Mayer, 1968, https://en.wikipedia.org/wiki/2001%3A_A_Space_Odyssey.

2 Redefining Capitalism in Global Economic Development, *Chapter 5 – Capitalism and Socialism: Sustainability Versus Popularity*, Kui-Wai Li, ScienceDirect Topics, 2017, https://www.sciencedirect.com/topics/economics-econometrics-and-finance/economic-growth.

3 An Inquiry into the Nature and Causes of the Wealth of Nations, Adam Smith, W. Strahan and T. Cadell, London, 1776.

4 Why Nations Fail: The Origins of Power, Prosperity, and Poverty, Daron Acemoglu, James A. Robinson, Crown Publishers, 2012, https://www.amazon.com/Why-Nations-Fail-Origins-Prosperity/dp/0307719219/.

5 The Innovation Delusion: How Our Obsession with the New Has Disrupted the Work That Matters Most, Lee Vinsel, Andrew L. Russell, Currency, 2020, https://www.amazon.com/Innovation-Delusion-Obsession-Disrupted-Matters/dp/0525575685/.

6 *Extinction: The Facts*, David Attenborough, BBC Studios, UK, 2020, https://en.wikipedia.org/wiki/Extinction:_The_Facts.

7 Capitalism, Socialism, and Democracy, Joseph A. Schumpeter, George Allen & Unwin Publishers Ltd., 1942, https://www.amazon.com/Capitalism-Socialism-Democracy-Joseph-Schumpeter/dp/0415107628/

8 The Innovator's Dilemma: When New Technologies Cause Great Firms to Fail, Clayton M. Christensen, Harvard Business School Press, 1997, https://www.amazon.com/Innovators-Dilemma-1st-first/dp/B0076ZFPKW.

9 What is Outcome-Driven Innovation?, Anthony Ulwick, Strategyn, 2014, https://strategyn.com/white-papers/what-is-outcome-driven-innovation/.

10 *THE 17 GOALS*, United Nations Department of Economic and Social Affairs, Sustainable Development, 2015, https://sdgs.un.org/goals.

11 "World fails to meet a single target to stop destruction of nature – UN report", Patrick Greenfield, Environment, *The Guardian*, 15 September 2020, https://www.theguardian.com/environment/2020/sep/15/every-global-target-to-stem-destruction-of-nature-by-2020-missed-un-report-aoe.

12 Global Biodiversity Outlook 5, Convention on Biological Diversity, United Nations Environment Programme, 2020, https://www.cbd.int/gbo5.

[13] "How to create an innovation strategy that translates to the operational team level", Mike Pinder: Innovation Expertise Lead, Author, & International Keynote Speaker, Board of Innovation, 05 December 2019, https://www.mikepinder.co.uk/2019/12/create-innovation-strategy-translates-operational-team-level/.

[14] Reinventing Organizations: A Guide to Creating Organizations Inspired by the Next Stage in Human Consciousness, Frederic Laloux, Nelson Parker, 2014, https://www.amazon.com/Reinventing-Organizations-Creating-Inspired-Consciousness-dp-296013351X/dp/296013351X/.

[15] 2020 Global 100 ranking, Corporate Knights, 21 January 2020, https://www.corporateknights.com/reports/2020-global-100/2020-global-100-ranking-15795648/.

[16] Reimagining Capitalism in a World on Fire, Rebecca Henderson, PublicAffairs, April 2020, https://www.amazon.com/Reimagining-Capitalism-World-Rebecca-Henderson/dp/1541730151.

[17] Circular Economy, McKinsey & Company, Sustainability, 2020, https://www.mckinsey.com/business-functions/sustainability/how-we-help-clients/circular-economy.

[18] Scale360° Circular Innovation, World Economic Forum, 2020, https://www.weforum.org/scale360-circular-innovation.

[19] The circular economy: Moving from theory to practice, Special edition, Michael T. Borruso, Venetia Simcock, Cait Murphy, Josh Resenfield, McKinsey Center for Business and Environment, October 2016, https://www.mckinsey.com/business-functions/sustainability/our-insights/the-circular-economy-moving-from-theory-to-practice.

CHAPTER 9
INFLECTIONS OF HOPE

Anthony Mills

A Sea Change of Perspective and Culture

As we gaze out across the horizon, there are very clear and positive signs of hope to be seen all around us. And while there have undoubtedly been scores, if not hundreds, of individual contributions to what now seems to be an overwhelming sea change of perspective and culture about the role of businesses – and governments – in the world, there have been, I believe, two particularly important and meaningful inflection points – and one significant inflection curve – in this whole sea change.

Inflection Point 1: 2006 – The B Corp Movement

To live is the rarest thing in the world. Most people exist, that is all.[1]

Oscar Wilde – Nineteenth Century Irish Poet and Playwright

I believe the <u>very first</u> true inflection point of this massive sea change of *perspective* and *culture* took place back in **2006**, when three friends – Jay Coen Gilbert, Bart Houlahan, and Andrew Kassoy – left their careers in business and private equity and created a brand new organization – **B Lab** (a non-profit) – dedicated solely to making it easier for mission-driven companies to protect and improve their <u>positive impacts</u> over time.

This was the start of the ***B Corp movement***.[2]

Since that time, B Corporations (for 'Benefit Corporation') have been accelerating a global culture shift to <u>redefine</u> **success in business** and build a more **inclusive** and **sustainable** economy all over the world.

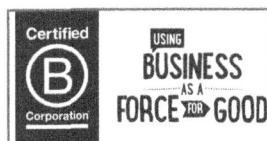

Certified B Corporations are businesses who meet a very high standard of verified social and environmental performance, public transparency, and legal accountability – all in the name of balancing purpose and profit.

The first cohort of B Corps – 82 in all – were certified the following year, in 2007 – truly anchoring and cementing the movement for all who would follow.

Becoming certified as a B Corp involves a comprehensive **assessment** of the overall business – not just its products and services – but precisely how the company itself is managed to ensure an overall positive impact on the world – which, according to B Labs, is what people ultimately care about.

More specifically, certified B Corporations must achieve a minimum verified score on the *B Impact Assessment*—a rigorous assessment of a company's impact on its workers, customers, community, and environment – and make their *B Impact Report* transparent on bcorporation.net. Certified B Corporations also amend their *legal governing documents* to require their board of directors to balance purpose and profit. B Corp Certification is fully administered by the non-profit B Lab.[3]

This combination of third-party validation, public transparency, and legal accountability enables Certified B Corps to build trust and value within and across their spheres of influence around the world.

B Corps believe that: "society's most challenging problems cannot be solved by government and nonprofits alone. The B Corp community thus works toward reduced inequality, lower levels of poverty, a healthier environment, stronger communities, and the creation of more high quality jobs with dignity and purpose. By harnessing the power of business, B Corps use profits and growth as a means to a greater end: positive impact for their employees, communities, and the environment."[4]

B Corps have furthermore formed a community of leaders driving a global movement of people striving to use business as a force for good. The values and aspirations of the B Corp community are consequently embedded in the *B Corp Declaration of Interdependence*, which bears reflecting here.[5]

The B Corp Declaration Of Interdependence

We envision a global economy that uses business as a force for good.

This economy is comprised of a new type of corporation – the B Corporation – which is purpose-driven and creates benefit for all stakeholders, not just shareholders.

As B Corporations and leaders of this emerging economy, we believe:

- *That we must be the change we seek in the world.*

- *That all business ought to be conducted as if people and place mattered.*

- *That, through their products, practices, and profits, businesses should aspire to do no harm and benefit all.*

- *To do so requires that we act with the understanding that we are each dependent upon another and thus responsible for each other and future generations.*

The B Corp movement has furthermore gone on to define what it refers to as the **B Economy**, described as follows:[6]

The B Economy

People don't believe the existing economic system is working for them. They're angry, and they're right. That's why we're working to build a B Economy that works for everyone, for the long term.

In the B Economy, businesses compete to be best for the world, the people living in it, and the natural environment on which our quality of life depends.

To build a B Economy, we need a new kind of business that balances purpose and profit. B Corporations are businesses that are legally required to consider the impact of their decisions on their workers, customers, community, and environment. Certified B Corporations have met the highest standards of verified performance and transparency.

The B Economy is bigger than B Corps. B Lab collaborates with leaders across all sectors of society to build a broader global movement of people using business as a force for good.

The B Economy is built by everyone who works for, buys from, invests in, learns or teaches about, or supports businesses striving to create a shared and durable prosperity for all. Join us.

Today, there are over 2,500 B Corps all over the world, and include such well-known – mostly midsized – businesses as Patagonia, Ben & Jerry's, Allbirds, Danone NA, Cabot Creamery, New Belgium Brewing, Seventh Generation, Cascade Engineering, and hundreds of others.

It is largely <u>these companies</u> who have been – and <u>continue to be</u> – the true **pioneers** – and **mavericks** if we may – in the business world leading the charge for balanced purpose and profit.

Not surprisingly, a number of companies involved in **'controversial' industries** have approached B Lab about becoming certified as B Corps, and B Labs has had to lean on its ***Standards Advisory Council***[7] to render various decisions regarding these businesses' eligibility for B Corp certifications.[8] This is largely on account of the types of artifacts (products and services) these businesses provide. Examples of some of these controversial industries have included:

- The Prison Industry
- The Casino Industry
- The Bottled Water Industry
- The Zoos, Aquariums, and Animal Parks Industry
- Private Banking in Switzerland
- Whole Life Insurance Products
- Cannabis-Related Products
- Breastmilk Substitutes
- Debt Collection Agencies in Emerging Markets
- Engineering Consulting Companies with Clients in the Defense Sector

B Lab and its Standards Advisory Council obviously take such inquiries on a case-by-case basis.

Inflection Point 2: 2015 – United Nations' SDGs

The arc of the moral universe is long, but it bends toward justice.

Dr. Martin Luther King Jr. – "Remaining Awake Through a Great Revolution", speech given at the National Cathedral, 31 March 1968[9], paraphrasing Unitarian clergyman Theodore Parker's sermon "Of Justice and the Conscience".[10]

I believe the second true inflection point of this massive sea change of *perspective* and *culture* took place in **September of 2015** when the **United Nations** was successful in getting all of its member states to ratify, and therefore adopt, the seventeen *Sustainable Development Goals* (*SDGs*) set forth in the *United Nations 2030 Agenda for Sustainable Development*.

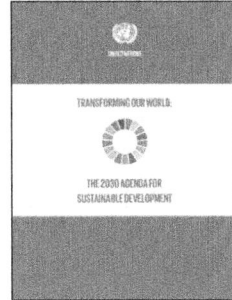

These were built upon – and further extensions of – the *Millennium Development Goals* (*MDGs*) that the UN member nations had previously committed to achieving by 2015.

These new Sustainable Development Goals dealt not only with *environmental sustainability*, but just as importantly, with *societal sustainability*, and therefore with equity and justice across all of society.

What the United Nations rightfully understood in this (renewed) movement was that ***business sustainability*** – of **all businesses** – is inherently **tied to**, and therefore **dependent upon**, ***societal*** and ***environmental sustainability***.

This is precisely why the theme of this Agenda was **"Leave No One Behind"**… no individual… no business… and no nation (and by extension its government). And it is why this new understanding – this *awakening* if we may – was such a pivotal inflection point for society overall.

IT'S 2015. NOW WHAT?

The new post-2015 development agenda builds on the Millennium Development Goals, eight anti-poverty targets that the world committed to achieving by 2015. Enormous progress has been made on the MDGs, showing the value of a unifying agenda underpinned by goals and targets. Yet despite this success, the indignity of poverty has not been ended for all.

The proposed framework has 17 Goals and 169 targets:

SUSTAINABLE DEVELOPMENT GOALS

PARTNERSHIPS FOR THE GOALS · PEACE & JUSTICE · LIFE ON LAND · LIFE BELOW WATER · PROTECT THE PLANET · RESPONSIBLE CONSUMPTION · SUSTAINABLE CITIES & COMMUNITIES · REDUCED INEQUALITIES · INNOVATION & INFRASTRUCTURE · GOOD JOBS & ECONOMIC GROWTH · CLEAN ENERGY · CLEAN WATER & SANITATION · GENDER EQUALITY · QUALITY EDUCATION · GOOD HEALTH · NO HUNGER · NO POVERTY

The United Nations summit for the adoption of the post-2015 development agenda will be held from Sept. 25 to 27, 2015, in New York and convened as a high-level plenary meeting of the General Assembly.

SOURCE: SUSTAINABLEDEVELOPMENT.UN.ORG

Inflection Point 3: 2016 – The Paris Agreement

Domini est terra et plenitudo eius orbis terrarium...
The earth is the Lord's and everything in it, the world and all who
live in it.

King David – A Psalm of David[11]

I believe the third true inflection point of this massive sea change of
perspective and *culture* also took place in **2015**, and was likewise spurred by
the **United Nations**.

This was when 196 state parties came together
under the umbrella of the ***United Nations***
Framework Convention on Climate Change
(***UNFCCC***) to negotiate the terms and language
of a new accord on climate change action to be taken by UN member states.
The specific actions involved were aimed at greenhouse-gas *emissions*
mitigation, climate-change *adaptation*, and climate-change *finance*.[12]

The final accord – dubbed **'The Paris Climate Agreement'** –
was reached at the UNFCCC's 21st *Conference of the Parties*
in Le Bourget (near Paris) and adopted by consensus on
12 December 2015.

It was subsequently signed in 2016 by all but two UN
member states (Iran and Turkey). Of major significance
was the fact that both China and India (two of the world's
worst CO_2 emitters) were signatories to the Agreement,
thus swaying numerous other countries to participate as
well.[13]

In June of 2017, the Trump Administration of the United States announced its
intentions to pull out of the Agreement – starting in November of 2020, just
before the end of the President's 2016 term. In practice however, changes in
US policy that were very contrary to the Paris Agreement were already put into
place well before that date.

The Paris Climate Agreement was <u>highly significant</u> in that it was the world's <u>very first</u> **comprehensive** climate agreement. Unfortunately, it is also a somewhat <u>fragile</u> agreement in that <u>none</u> of the commitments of its member nations are <u>legally binding</u> upon them (unlike with the Agreement's predecessor, the Kyoto Protocol of 1997), though they are 'politically encouraged' (a practice sometimes known as 'name and shame').

While the Agreement contained no terms **forcing** member nations to set <u>specific emissions targets</u> by <u>specific dates</u>, it did stipulate that each nations' target had to <u>exceed</u> that which it had previously set <u>prior to the Agreement</u> (what it called 'ambitious' *Nationally Determined Contributions*, or *NDCs*). It also pressed the member states to take actions to reduce their emissions **as quickly as possible**, so as to achieve "a balance between anthropogenic emissions by sources, and removals by sinks of greenhouse gases" in the second half of the 21st Century. As such, the Agreement tasked each member nation with determining and planning its specific actions, and thereafter regularly reporting on those actions and their impacts to the UN.[14]

The ultimate **<u>aim</u>** of the Paris Climate Agreement was to **limit** <u>long-term global average temperature change</u> (in other words, to limit the potential for unchecked global warming).

More specifically, as per the Agreement's **Article 2** – "enhancing the implementation" of the UNFCCC – the aim was **<u>three-fold</u>**:[15]

1. Holding the <u>increase</u> in the global average temperature to well below 2°C above pre-industrial levels and to pursue efforts to limit the temperature increase to 1.5°C above pre-industrial levels, recognizing that this would significantly <u>reduce</u> the *risks* and *impacts* of climate change;

2. Increasing the ability to <u>adapt</u> to the *adverse impacts* of climate change and foster *climate resilience* and low greenhouse gas emissions development, in a manner that does not threaten food production;

3. Making finance flows consistent with a pathway towards low greenhouse gas emissions and climate-resilient development (in other words, <u>financially incentivize</u> private actors to help the nations move in this direction, through various policy and national economic actions).

This approach involved establishing somewhat specific energy and climate **policies**, including the so-called **20/20/20 targets** – the reduction of carbon dioxide (CO_2) emissions by 20%, the increase of renewable energy's market share to 20%, and a 20% increase in energy efficiency – all of which, when pursued "as soon as possible" (expediting the "global peaking of greenhouse gas emissions" as the Agreement called for) would serve as a major incentive for divestment away from fossil fuels and towards renewable energy sources.

The Agreement also called for a global **stocktake** every 5 years – to assess the collective progress being made towards achieving the aims of the Agreement and to inform further individual actions by the respective parties.

Not surprisingly, the Paris Climate Agreement faced its share of **criticism**, most notably because it contained no binding *enforcement mechanisms* to measure and control CO_2 emissions, and because there were no specific *penalties* or *fiscal pressures* included – such as a *carbon tax* or other type of *emissions tax* – to discourage bad behaviors and/or inaction (though such measures could be integrated into individual countries' NDCs).[16]

There has also been some criticism that the Agreement's *carbon accounting* – based on the CMIP5 climate model – would result in insufficient GHG emissions to achieve it stated temperature-change targets. Indeed, in the period since the Agreement was signed, the world has seen the hottest years on record to date, with 19 of the 20 hottest years having all occurred since 2001, with the year 2016 ranking as the warmest on record as of this writing.[17], [18], [19]

But despite its inherent weaknesses, the Paris Climate Agreement remains an important *inflection point* in the **global consciousness** toward overall *planetary sustainability*, and as such, history will without a doubt note the role that it has played in this sea change of *perspective* and *culture*.

Inflection Point 4: 2019 – Business Roundtable

We're here to put a dent in the universe. Otherwise why even be here.

Steve Jobs – paraphrase taken from a 1985 interview.[20, 21]

I believe the fourth (reinforcing) inflection point of this sea change of *perspective* and *culture* took place in **August of 2019,** when **Business Roundtable** – a consortium of mostly Fortune 500 CEOs, led at the time by such business luminaries as Jamie Dimon, Chairman and CEO of JPMorgan Chase & Co., and Alex Gorsky, Chairman of the Board and Chief Executive Officer of Johnson & Johnson – released a new ***Statement on the Purpose of a Corporation*** declaring that the true purpose of a corporation was not simply to serve its *shareholders*, but rather to serve all of society, and thus all stakeholders who are in any way impacted by the corporation's behaviors.[22]

This new statement was co-signed by 181 Chief Executive Officers, every one of whom made a clear commitment to leading their companies for the benefit of all stakeholders – customers, employees, suppliers, communities, and shareholders. Communities here also included these communities' respective environments, and this commitment thus extended to the environment as well, and to the pursuit of sustainable practices that benefit the environment. This declaration carried great weight on account of the massive size of many of the companies involved – companies like Apple, Amazon, IBM, and others.

Later on – in **October** of that same year - very similar sentiments and rationales were echoed by Marc Benioff, CEO of Salesforce, when he boldly declared that the world needed **"A New Capitalism"**.[23] Therein, Benioff asserted that, "The current system has led to profound inequality. To fix it, we need businesses and executives to value purpose alongside profit."[24]

This – I believe – was the ultimate turning point where the world finally woke up and understood what was taking place right before them, which was, namely, that our world was becoming one in which purpose – of both businesses and individuals – mattered more than did pure profit... that both businesses and individuals were put here on this planet to live out some true purpose in the world; in other words... to be purpose-driven.

Of course, to give **credit** where credit is due, much of this sentiment <u>predated</u> Business Roundtable's 2019 declaration and had already been embodied in the corporate governance model of the *B Corporation* (Benefit Corporation), whose corporate governance model – known as 'benefit corporation governance' – inherently places workers, customers, suppliers, communities, and the environment at its core, right alongside, and with equal weight to (if not more weight than) that of shareholders.

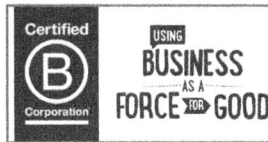

It is largely due to the pioneering work of these B Corps – a movement that began back in 2006 – that the major corporations named in the Business Roundtable declaration finally felt the <u>public pressure</u> to make this deciding move themselves.

History is still watching to judge whether or not these CEOs and their companies will fully live up to this pledge the way that the Certified B Corporations have.

Inflection Curve 1 – Sustainable Financing

> *We started considering issuing green bonds due to investors asking about this, and the clamor got louder, so we couldn't ignore it!*
>
> **Mark Merrigan – National Treasury Management Agency, Ireland**[25]

I believe the one real **inflection curve** mirroring this massive sea change of *perspective* and *culture* in the world has been the undisputable rise of **sustainable infrastructure financing** practices.

This overarching **trend** has done more by itself to facilitate the realization of the UN's *Sustainable Development Goals* and the aims of the *2016 Paris Climate Agreement* than perhaps anything else in this recent period of history.

It is therefore worth taking a detailed look at.

The Rise of Sustainable Infrastructure Financing[26]

Given the general nature of infrastructure for the *public good*, and the positive externalities that its facilities typically generate – infrastructure investments have traditionally been financed using public funds, with **governments** being their main facilitators.

However, in many economies very real situations like increased public debt to GDP ratios, public deficits, and the inability of the public sector to deliver efficient investment spending have led to a **reduction** in the level of public funds available for, and thus being allocated to, **infrastructure development**.

In some cases, budgetary pressures have been further compounded by the need to rebuild bank balance sheets and capital and liquidity buffers, arising in part out of stronger banking sector regulations following the Great Recession.

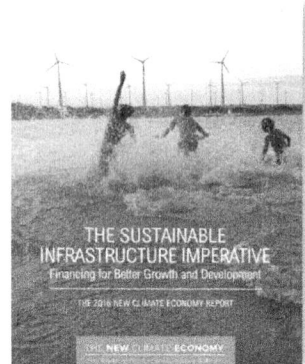

Consequently, it has become increasingly acknowledged that **alternative sources of financing** are absolutely <u>necessary</u> for supporting infrastructure development needs and meet the many <u>ongoing</u> <u>unmet</u> infrastructure needs all over the world.

It was for this reason that over the second decade of the Twenty-First Century, the world witnessed incredible growth in the use of **'sustainable financing'** for certain new infrastructure development projects around the world.

In particular, ***sustainable infrastructure financing*** refers to the use of specialized alternative financial instruments and mechanisms to finance select 'social' and 'green' infrastructure projects all over the world.

The use of these instruments and mechanisms witnessed substantial growth in the 2010s. Since that time they have been used extensively to finance projects in emerging markets all over the world, where mature capital markets – with the scale and capacity that large developed markets have – often simply <u>do not exist</u>. They have also been used to finance 'green' projects that are focused squarely on various aspects of environmental sustainability.

It is in this context, then, that attention has increasingly turned to **institutional investors**, given the long-term nature of the liabilities used for most types of institutional investment, and the corresponding need for suitable long-term assets. **However**, for a wide range of reasons, including a lack of familiarity with infrastructure investment, *institutional investors* have traditionally allocated only a <u>very small</u> fraction of their investments to infrastructure projects, and when they <u>have</u> invested in such projects, it has generally been through listed companies and fixed income instruments, rather than through <u>direct investment</u>.

However – as came to be seen in the 2010s – infrastructure <u>can</u> be financed through a <u>wide range</u> of (very innovative) capital channels, using a very <u>broad range</u> of financial instruments and structures. Some – like listed stocks and bonds – are <u>market-based</u>, with very well-established regulatory frameworks. And of course there have always been standard infrastructure <u>loans</u>, which have traditionally been underwritten by commercial banks.

But in more recent years, efforts have been made to develop even newer and more innovative financial instruments and techniques for financing infrastructure development – in many cases with excellent success, but also not without a noticeable learning curve.

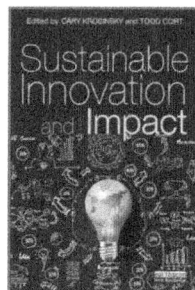

All of this notwithstanding, some investors have persisted in the perception that there are an inadequate array of appropriate financing structures. Typically, only the largest investors have had the capacity to invest directly in infrastructure projects. Smaller pension funds and other similar funds have generally had to use pooled investment vehicles to access this market. Collective investment vehicles have been available, such as infrastructure funds, but problems like high fees, mismatches between asset life and fund vehicle, and extensive leverage have meant that these options were not always palatable to all investors. Consequently, the market has evolved to address many of these concerns. For example, several unlisted equity funds emerged in the market offering longer investment terms, something that several important bond funds also now do.

Clearly, this situation has been far more dire in developing markets than it has in developed markets. Global challenges like urbanization, population growth, shifting geopolitical conditions, fluctuating commodities prices, and climate change are generally felt far more keenly in emerging markets than they are in developed markets.

Ironically, **infrastructure** is often the **key asset** that such emerging markets need in order to attain the regional and domestic *market stability* required to address and overcome most of these challenges, as well as to achieve the robust economic growth and development needed to enable their economies to make the most of opportunities standing before them.

Fortunately, these innovative new financing mechanisms and instruments have seen – and continue to see – rapid, mainstream adoption in the world.

Primary Drivers of Sustainable Infrastructure Financing

The primary **drivers** behind **sustainable infrastructure financing** have been:

1. Since the start of the Twenty-First Century, infrastructure **needs** in all markets, but especially in emerging markets, have far <u>outpaced</u> the traditional levels of development in those markets, with power generation in particular accounting for more than half of the needed investment (much of which has continued to remain <u>unmet</u>).

2. Most **governments** lack access to adequate capital to finance **all** of their infrastructure needs at any given time. Thus their traditional financing mechanisms are <u>inadequate</u> to keep pace with the scope of needs they are responsible for addressing.

3. **Institutional investors** have become increasingly <u>aware of</u> the potential to make a positive return on infrastructure investments, and are drawn to infrastructure because it represents an opportunity to <u>diversify</u> their portfolios and secure interest rate and inflation <u>protections</u>, all while helping to contribute to <u>public goals</u>. Amongst these tend to be sovereign wealth funds, pension funds, asset managers, and insurance companies.

4. There is furthermore the opportunity to invest in well-defined, highly-transparent, and well-managed **'green' funds** that not only support infrastructure development per se, but more importantly support the development of assets that serve to promote environmental and social **sustainability** in various places around the world, thus meeting many investors' *Environmental, Social, and Governance* (ESG) objectives.

Key Trends in Sustainable Infrastructure Financing

Continued Gap Growth in Infrastructure Needs

For many years now, there has been an ongoing **urgent need** for infrastructure investments, especially in emerging markets. According to McKinsey Global Institute, the world would have to invest 3.8% of global GDP – USD 3.3T – each year through 2030 to meet all needs, with emerging markets accounting for about 60% of the total need.[27]

This means that, taken together, emerging markets would be able to absorb **USD 2T** per year in infrastructure spending, about half of which has continued to go unmet. Moreover, the gap has continued to grow. McKinsey Global Institute noted in 2018 that if the then-current rate of underinvestment were to continue, the shortfall will be 11%, or USD 350B, each year. Moreover, if the additional investment required to meet the UN's *Sustainable Development Goals* (SDGs) were included, the size of that gap would triple.[28]

Some of the regions witnessing the greatest needs in this area have generally been East Asia and Sub-Saharan Africa. Sub-Saharan Africa in particular has needs that far outpace the size of its economies, and consequently suffers from massive under-investment, with the World Bank estimating an infrastructure financing gap of USD 93B per year in that region.

A Major Market Shift in Infrastructure Financing Channels – From Corporate Finance to Project Finance and Co-Investment[29]

Historically speaking, ***corporate finance*** was the predominant channel used to finance private infrastructure. For example, private investment in regulated entities like utilities has an extremely long track record, typically carried on the books of the companies themselves. This has been the case in other sectors as well, such as seaports, oil and gas, waste, and electricity generation.

Numerous companies in these sectors – the providers of these infrastructure services – are in fact quite large corporations listed on public exchanges, and own quite sizeable infrastructure assets involved in delivering these services. Consequently, they have been investors in the associated infrastructure projects. They range from specialist businesses to diversified conglomerates.

In more recent times however, infrastructure financing has increasingly taken on the form of pure *project finance*, owing largely to growing budgetary constraints. This approach has emerged as the go-to financial solution for infrastructure involving public entities acting in the role of either regulator or counterparty. In particular, project finance has become a very popular method for attracting private capital, most notably investment in projects characterized by high specificity, high capital-intensity, and low re-deployable value.

As a result, the market witnessed the evolution of various **co-investment platforms** – to leverage institutional investors' capital in such *project finance* alongside other sources. The main driver for the creation of these mechanisms was the recognition that not all investors necessarily had the resources and expertise to make direct investments in infrastructure projects, but yet they had the investible capital, while other investors had in fact built significant scale and market presence there, together with the expertise needed to perform proper due diligence on infrastructure projects. Such co-investment platforms thus pool investor capital to deploy directly into infrastructure projects, bypassing traditional intermediaries like banks and investment managers. This trend was reinforced by large funds seeking to reduce the cost of infrastructure investment, and to align internal governance and portfolio management models with direct infrastructure investments.

Consequently there has come to be, in recent years, a **wide range** of **financing channels** for infrastructure investment – both direct and market-based – each with its own characteristics and implications. But market-based financing has been the most popular, given its numerous attractive benefits, not the least of which has been regulatory protections and attractive returns.

Historical Infrastructure Financing Mechanisms[30]

Historically-speaking, debt has represented about three-fourths of total private infrastructure financing, with loans being about 1.5 times the size of bonds. Before 2008, international loans had been the main infrastructure funding source, but following that year, international lending slowed and local loans and bonds tended to fill in the gap. International instruments did rebound in 2013, though this was largely due to a few major transactions in limited sectors in Mexico, China, and Brazil. Inevitably the tide between local and international loans will always ebb and flow to some degree, depending on other global factors.

Newer Funding <u>Mechanisms</u> Being Used for Emerging Markets[31]

Since the start of the Twenty-First Century, three new forms of funding have arisen for financing infrastructure in <u>emerging markets</u>. These have been important <u>alternatives</u> to traditional commercial bank loans.

These new mechanisms were:

1. **Multilateral Development Finance Institutions** (M-DFIs) – such as *African Development Bank* (*AfDB*) of Ivory Coast;

2. **Bilateral Development Finance Institutions** (B-DFIs) – such as *Overseas Private Investment Corporation* (*OPIC*) of the United States; and...

3. **Export Credit Agencies** (ECAs) – such as *Etihad Credit Insurance* of the United Arab Emirates.

Over time a shift was seen in the balance between these mechanisms, especially between multilateral and bilateral DFIs, with increased usage of bilateral lending, and a correspondingly lowered use of multilateral lending.

The shift away from multilaterals may not remain forever however. Tackling such massive issues as global climate change by their <u>very nature</u> require the cooperation of <u>numerous parties</u> working together <u>multilaterally</u>. Thus, as more and more emphasis continues to be placed on environmental and other forms of *sustainability*, there can always be a shift back toward multilaterals.

In some cases, Multilateral DFIs, Bilateral DFIs, ECAs, and commercial banks have all cooperated <u>together</u> in a <u>complementary manner</u> to fill out the totality of infrastructure financing needs in these markets. But DFIs have tended to carry the brunt of the risk in those situations.

Private Sector Participation in Infrastructure Financing[32, 33]

While there have been significant <u>increases</u> over the years in bilateral and multilateral policy investments, these have **never been** – and **never will be** – **enough** to meet the **overall need** inside of emerging markets. Other sources of funding have been needed as well, and in particular much more *private capital* has been needed, and thus sought out.

Historically speaking, government budgets were the largest source of funds for infrastructure financing, accounting for about 75% of all infrastructure dollars spent, with the private sector providing the balance. But following the Great Recession, governments witnessed their fiscal deficits grow and their budgets shrink, greatly expanding the need for private funding. Most private funding, however, has traditionally flowed to upper middle-income countries, and **not** to emerging markets. Consequently, while government finances around the world have remained under pressure, nowhere has this been truer than in emerging markets. According to the *International Monetary Fund*, public debt in emerging markets and middle-income economies hovers close to 50% of GDP. And for low-income developing countries, average debt-to-GDP ratios have climbed at a rapid pace, and actually exceeded **40%** following 2017.

Thus, given institutional investors attraction to the infrastructure market (for the reasons cited above), and despite their traditionally small allocation to this market, private infrastructure investments have in fact increasingly attracted the **attention** of institutional investors. Not surprisingly, more of these investors have entered this space through debt, co-investment platforms, and other secondaries, than have through direct investment.

Green Financing[34, 35, 36, 37, 38, 39, 40, 41, 42]

A very notable trend in infrastructure financing has been the rapidly growing emphasis in more recent times on ***sustainability***, which is generally looked at very holistically – with focus being placed on *social*, *environmental*, and *local economic* impacts, as well as an increased emphasis on things like *local materials*, *local workers*, and other *cultural sensitivities*. In general, managing the risks associated with local stakeholders has been seen as increasingly important to the overall pursuit of infrastructure sustainability.

Consequently, there have come to be increasing environmental and social provisions being made inside of DFI loans – a trend that is expected to continue indefinitely. This has given rise to the use of so-called ***Green Bonds***, which in some cases even have interest payments payable in climate credits instead of in direct cash.

THE WORLD BANK

1O YEARS OF GREEN BONDS

FROM EVOLUTION TO REVOLUTION

In particular, **China's commitment** to the **2016 Paris Agreement** was seen as pivotal point in this movement, and further influenced other countries to follow suit and thereby create even more momentum for *Green Bonds*.

Green Bonds are fixed income securities (just like regular bonds) whose proceeds are used to finance clearly specified new or existing eligible 'green projects' – projects that create real and sustainable environmental impact, such as in combating pollution, climate change, and the depletion of biodiversity and natural resources – together with a high level of transparency. Green Bonds are either asset-backed or asset-linked, and issuers have to declare the types of green projects eligible to receive their funds at issuance. Green Bonds are the largest instrument in the broader universe of socially responsible investments, which include bonds and equities from issuers identified by *Environmental, Social, and Governance* (ESG) standards.

Issuance of Green Bonds grew extremely rapidly in the 2010s, rising from less than **USD 50B** in **2014** to almost **USD 255B** in **2019**. A key catalyst for this was the 2014 introduction of the *Green Bond Principles* (GBPs) by the *International Capital Market Association* (ICMA). The GBPs govern: (i) the use of proceeds; (ii) the process for project evaluation and selection; (iii) the management of proceeds; and (iv) reporting. Bonds that meet the GBPs or, alternatively, the Climate Bond Initiative's (CBI) *Climate Bonds Standard* (CBS) are eligible for green bond certification by either third-party providers or the CBI. Certification gives investors assurance that the bonds confer environmental or climate-related benefits, helping to safeguard against so-called 'greenwashing'.

Green Bonds, in fact, became so popular amongst socially-conscious investors in the late 2010s that even large multinational corporations like **Apple**, **Microsoft**, and **Ford Motor Company** jumped onto the bandwagon and began investing in Green Bonds.[43, 44, 45] This undoubtedly spurred even more likeminded MNCs to follow in their steps. Indeed, Microsoft's actions were part of a larger consortium focused on reducing carbon emissions that included such MNCs as Nike, Starbucks, Unilever NV, and Danone SA.[46]

In terms of the types of projects financed by Green Bonds (at the time of this writing), renewable energy and green buildings have experienced the largest share of total issuance – 31% and 29%, respectively. Clean transport projects also have steadily increased over the years as a percentage of issuance. Adaptation projects have represented only a small portion of overall projects, at 1% of total issuance, along with projects pertaining to land use at 4%.

Public-Private Partnerships – Beyond Financing[47, 48, 49, 50, 51, 52, 53, 54, 55]

Ever since the 1990s, there has been a growing trend – starting first in Europe, the UK, and Australia, then Canada and the United States, and since then in many other places around the world – to employ **Public-Private Partnerships** (**PPPs**, or **P3s**) to not only <u>finance</u> major infrastructure assets, but also to <u>design</u>, <u>build</u>, <u>operate</u>, and <u>maintain</u> such assets over an <u>extended lifecycle</u>.

A Public-Private Partnership is a long-term contract between a government entity and a private party (including in some cases consortia of multiple private parties) for providing a **public asset** or **service**, in which the private party bears significant risk and management responsibility, and remuneration is linked to the <u>operational performance</u> of the asset. These differ from traditional service contracts and turnkey construction contracts, which are categorized as public procurement projects, and from the privatization of utilities, where there is a very limited ongoing role for the public sector. P3s are quite often used for large, complex projects like airports, seaports, power-generation stations, wastewater treatment facilities, solid waste treatment facilities, major highway systems, and citywide parking services. They are also used increasingly for such <u>service-intensive</u> infrastructure as prisons, hospitals, schools, university housing, and sports complexes.

P3s have been favored in many cases because they allow governments to institute new infrastructure assets <u>without</u> having to finance them upfront themselves (and therefore without having to raise the financing). By their nature, the private party generally makes the upfront investment in the asset and then recoups this (usually with a generous return) over the long run through the <u>operating contract</u> for the asset, which generally tend to be 15, 20, 25, 30, 40, and even 50 years in duration, with some even going to 100 years.

P3s have many specific **pros** and **cons**.

One of the major **pros** of P3s has been that because the private party has to operate and maintain the asset over most or all of its lifecycle, there is greater 'ownership mentality' involved, which tends to drive better, more innovative, and more operationally cost-effective designs and constructions, when compared to design and construction that are simply contracted to a design & build firm with no vested interest once the project is completed.

One of the major **cons** of P3s has been that contractual terms – especially those around *non-compete clauses* – can significantly constrain what governments are at liberty to do in the future, lest they have to compensate the private party for lost revenues resulting from their actions. In the long run, this can significantly hamper future development in certain areas. Thus both sides have to be extremely careful in working out the contractual terms of the partnership, to ensure that it ends up being a win-win for both parties over the long run. This is especially true considering that in the period of time of the contract, technology, demographics, the environment, and politics will all inevitably change, and most such changes cannot be predicted with certainty.

Though actual data has been scant over the years, there has been clear evidence of the ongoing **growth** in the use of P3s around the world, much of which has been driven by the continued persistent **gap** in infrastructure needs – for both new and replacement infrastructure – and the **lack** of capital budgets within governments to meet those needs directly.

Consequently, more and more nations have instituted policies that encourage the use of P3s, to make more efficient use of capital while also supporting economic development through the private sector.

Some of the other important trends seen in the field of P3s have included:

- A growing emphasis on people – by looking at the P3's social, economic, and environmental impacts – influenced in part by the United Nations' *Sustainable Development Goals* (SDGs).

- A growing interest in sustainable, resilient, and regenerative P3s that can withstand, and recover from, natural / environmental strains over the long run.

- A surplus of maturing P3 projects, where governments then have to figure out how to manage assets being handed back over to them as their contracts reach maturity – assets that in many cases these governments have no experience in managing and operating.

- A growing number of legal reforms and frameworks focusing on better governance of P3s – designed to establish or improve the enabling environments for P3s. These have served to mitigate some of the legal constraints that otherwise caused developers and investors to historically avoid P3s in certain markets.

- A growing demand and push for more <u>transparent</u>, <u>competitive</u> procurement processes, often using e-procurement platforms to ensure transparency, and sometimes driven by the MDBs investing in the projects.

- A growing recognition of the need for – and thus a push to establish – P3 <u>centers of excellence</u> within governments designed to help grow these governments' skills and abilities in procuring, architecting, and operating P3s, so that they can be leveraged more broadly in a city, region, or nation.

- A growing focus on national <u>budget strategies</u>, <u>pipelines</u>, and <u>priorities</u>, so that there was full <u>visibility</u> into <u>all projects</u> under consideration, so that governments did not overcommit themselves to endeavors they could not realistically support.

- A growing understanding of P3s by <u>domestic banks</u> in emerging markets – a move that attracted these banks to invest in local P3s where governments might not otherwise be able to attract larger investors.

- A growing awareness amongst governments of the opportunity to market investment opportunities to attract <u>FDI</u> for P3s – including undertaking more thorough due diligence to prove the attractiveness of certain P3 projects to foreign investors.

- A decreasing tolerance for <u>unsolicited P3s</u> – typically the seed for nepotism and corruption in many places – replaced instead by very <u>clearly defined</u> and <u>transparent</u> public-procurement practices for P3s.

- The growing emergence of <u>P3 institutions</u> championing the value of P3s – in nations all over the world, various lobbying, advisory, and excellence centers have been established to help promote the adoption and use of P3s more broadly. This significantly bolstered the understanding of the value of P3s, as well as how to optimally structure and manage them, and consequently the appetite for leveraging P3s.

- A growing trend in Islamic nations to incorporate <u>Islamic finance</u> for the use of P3s.

Examples of Sustainable Infrastructure Financing

Multilateral DFI: Meridiam Used EBRD & MIGA To Finance Hospital[56]

The French investment firm Meridiam was the sponsor of a project for the financing of a hospital in Turkey. Meridiam used a *European Bank for Reconstruction and Development* (EBRD) Enhancement Facility and a *World Bank Multilateral Investment Guarantee Agency* (MIGA) political and contractual risk insurance to enable the financing of this project with a bond rated two notches above the sovereign.

Multilateral DFI: ADB's Credit Guarantee & Investment Facility[57]

Asian Development Bank (ADB), of Manilla, Philippines, uses a credit guarantee and investment facility that provides guarantees on local-currency-denominated bonds as evidence of its increased willingness to engage with stakeholders to improve the processes, and to innovate risk allocation in general. This is a clear example of how multilateral DFIs have become more customer-focused in recent years.

Multilateral DFI: AfDB Leveraged Hedge Funds Insurance[58]

In recent years the African Development Bank (AfDB) of Abidjan, Ivory Coast bought insurance on a USD 1B loan portfolio from hedge funds, thereby reducing the amount of capital held against these loans. This greatly freed up the bank's lending capacity so that it could service an even larger portfolio of projects in Sub-Saharan Africa, and thus help address the region's extensive ongoing infrastructure-funding gap.

ECA: Afreximbank Introduced EDF and Fast-Track PPF[59]

In recent years, Afreximbank of Cairo, Egypt introduced an African fund for export development to attract more private equity, as well as a project preparation facility (PPF) to address project development-related constraints. The PPF is designed to fast-track the supply of bankable projects and to crowd in private sector lenders so as to bridge financing gaps that exist in both project and infrastructure development.

Co-Investment: Freeport LNG Liquefaction Project[60]

Freeport LNG – located in Freeport, Texas – is a major center for natural gas liquefaction and transportation. It closed on USD 12.5B in debt and equity financing through 2015, making it the largest non-recourse construction project financing up to that point in time.

For the development of its second liquefaction production facility, a syndicate of 25 commercial banks provided approximately USD 4B over a seven-year construction term. Due to the exceptionally large size of this project, a large syndicate of lenders was necessary to secure the financing. The loan was structured for issuance to capital market investors.

Co-Investment: OMERS Global Strategic Investment Alliance – GSIA[61]

In 2012 the Ontario Municipal Employees Retirement System (OMERS) launched its own global co-investment alliance platform, known as the *Global Strategic Investment Alliance* – the *GSIA*. The GSIA was designed to gather sophisticated like-minded investors (mainly pension funds) to invest directly in infrastructure assets.

Through the GSIA, participating alliance members invest in core infrastructure assets with an enterprise value in excess of USD 2B in sectors such as airports, railways, ports, power generation & distribution, and gas pipelines, mainly in North America and Europe.

At its inception, the GSIA set out to raise USD 20B, with OMERS providing USD 5B of that. In April 2012 Mitsubishi Corporation entered into binding commitments to jointly invest up to USD 2.5B in quality infrastructure assets, together with leading Japanese pension funds and financial institutions, namely Pension Fund Association, Japan Bank for International Cooperation, and Mizuho Corporate Bank. In March 2014 OMERS entered into a co-investment agreement with Japan's Government Pension Investment Fund (GPIF), the world's largest pension fund, and the Development Bank of Japan (DBJ). The participation by GPIF and DBJ brought the total capital committed to the GSIA to USD 11.25B in 2015.

Green Bond: The IFC Forest Bond[62]

In October 2016, International Finance Corporation (IFC) – a member of the World Bank Group – announced that it had issued a first-of-its-kind *Green Bond* that gave investors the option of getting repaid in <u>either</u> carbon credits or cash, raising USD 152M to support private sector development and prevent deforestation in developing countries.

IFC saw halting deforestation as essential to meeting the global community's climate goal of keeping global warming under 2°C, while also offering an important opportunity to boost rural livelihoods and protect vital ecosystems in certain regions. But in order to do that, it needed to mobilize between USD 75B and 300B over the ensuing decade, much of which would need to come from the private sector. It thus issued the <u>IFC Forest Bond</u> – an instrument demonstrating the power of innovative capital-market mechanisms to unlock private sector funds for forest protection.

Investors were offered a choice between a cash or carbon-credit coupon. A carbon credit is a tradable certificate or permit representing the right to emit one ton of carbon dioxide or another greenhouse gas with an equivalent to one ton of carbon dioxide. Investors choosing the carbon credit coupon can retire the credits to offset corporate greenhouse gas emissions, or sell them on the carbon market.

This five-year bond was sold to major global institutional investors – including CalSTRS, Treehouse Investments LLC, TIAA-CREF, and QBE. Proceeds are to support IFC's private sector lending in emerging markets. The bond was listed on the London Stock Exchange.

To pay investors a carbon credit coupon, IFC will buy carbon credits from a project that follows the United Nations Reducing Emissions from Deforestation and Forest Degradation, or REDD, scheme. A REDD project offers economic incentives to reduce deforestation and invest in low-carbon growth. More specifically, the project from which IFC will purchase carbon credits is the Kasigau Corridor REDD project in Kenya. This project is operated by Wildlife Works, who enables tens of thousands of rural farmers in Kenya to benefit from voluntarily agreeing to protect an important migration corridor for endangered African elephants.

IFC developed the Forests Bond with BHP Billiton and Conservation International. BHP Billiton is a global mining, metals, and petroleum company. Conservation International is a global nonprofit environmental organization. BHP Billiton provides a price-support mechanism for the Forests Bond. If investors elect the cash coupon instead of the carbon coupon, BHP Billiton offtakes the carbon credits generated and delivered by the Kasigau Corridor REDD project. Conservation International helped to identify the project to be supported by the bond.

IFC has been one of the pioneers in the green bond market as well as in climate financing. It has raised climate finance through a variety of innovative instruments including billions in green bonds. Green bond proceeds are set aside and invested exclusively in climate-smart projects such as energy efficiency and renewable energy. As such, IFC is one of the world's largest financiers of climate-smart projects in developing countries, with climate-smart investments totaling over $13 billion over the last decade. As part of its Climate Implementation Plan, IFC has committed to lead efforts in catalyzing $13 billion a year in private sector capital for climate investment by 2020.

Green Bond: South Africa's Touwsrivier Solar Project Bond[63]

The Touwsrivier Solar Project Bond was a highly innovative example of using fixed income capital markets to finance an infrastructure project, especially given that South Africa has had a developing financial system with a growing base of institutional investors.

This bond was launched to finance the construction of a 44 MWp Concentrated Photovoltaic Plant in an economically impoverished part of the country, which also qualified it as a Green Bond.

The bond featured numerous innovative components, including:

- It was issued in the local currency with a face value of 1B ZAR.

- It was issued with a 15 year maturity and 11% coupon.

- It had an amortizing repayment structure similar to a mortgage – a highly innovative structure that effectively dealt with the risks of the typical bullet structure used in project bonds, namely their difficulty in adapting to project finance that can later on create a refinancing risk.

- Incentives through South Africa's REFIT program that allow national electric utilities to purchase power from renewable sources at predetermined prices through the backing of the South African Department of Energy, which had the effect of raising the credit quality of the issue. Consequently, the bond was rated Baa2 by Moody's at issuance.

P3 Bond: The United States Qualified Public Infrastructure Bonds[64]

In January 2015, the US Government proposed an innovative class of municipal bonds that benefit from existing tax exemptions to further spur private investment in infrastructure.

Called the *Qualified Public Infrastructure Bond*, or *QPIB*, these are a new entity in the bond market that extend the benefits of municipal bond finance to Public Private Partnerships (P3), providing supportive financing in transportation, airports, ports, sewer, and water. In effect, this opens up new channels of financing (namely taxable investors) to P3s, and can serve to reduce the overall cost of financing. To be eligible for a QPIB, projects must be owned by a state or local government and be available for general public use.

P3: The George Deukmejian Courthouse of Long Beach, California[65]

The largest availability-payment–based social infrastructure project in US history – the George Deukmejian Courthouse in Long Beach, California – represents a successful P3 that accelerated replacement of an outdated and poorly functioning facility. The state of California awarded the project to a private consortium in a 35-year project agreement. The building was completed in 2013, on time and within budget, and it opened in May 2014. For its part, the private consortium gained low-risk cash flow payments on the lease for the full duration, protected by the clause that the consortium can evict the state if availability payments are not made. Today, the state of California continues to occupy the award-winning courthouse, with dramatically improved facilities and amenities, room to expand, and a performance-based agreement with the concessionaire to ensure satisfactory long-term operations.

P3: Australia's Pacific Highway Upgrade[66]

When Australia's Roads and Maritime Services (then known as the Road Traffic Authority) needed to upgrade the nations' 657 kilometer Pacific Highway in 1996, it turned to a Public-Private Partnership to do so. When it began this undertaking, the highway's Ballina Bypass was one of its first projects. Building this roadway in New South Wales involved five different organizations providing design, contracting, and geotechnical services. This particular project was a major technical challenge because the road had to be built on soft ground. Moreover, RTA had a lot riding on the success of the Ballina Bypass because at the time such P3 contracts were very new in the country.

The five organizations were also new to working together, so they had to establish operating principles for the project by which they would work. They needed to continually demonstrate to RTA that they were working as an integrated team, sharing innovations, and solving steep technical problems as they arose (of which there were many).

The different organizations each appointed people to three roles to strengthen their working relationships: an alliance manager, the alliance leadership team, and the alliance management team. The teams then designated and trained functional experts to be leaders responsible for achieving key metrics in their areas. The functional experts communicated weekly on project status with the alliance leadership and management teams, and through fortnightly meetings, regular emails, and weekly site walks.

All this ensured the five organizations openly heard and resolved project problems together. The leadership training also enabled the functional experts to learn how to resolve issues constructively. One of these issues occurred near the end of the project, when the road builders had to add very expensive fill – even more than they originally projected – to shore up soft ground. All five partners accepted this reality, even though it pinched their profits, in keeping with the win-win / lose-lose principles they had set up for the partnership.

The end result was that they finished the work seven months ahead of schedule and for USD 100M less than estimated in the original concept design.

Our Job

Given all of these historical inflection points and inflection curve profiled here, the next logical question is... "Okay, what is our job in all of this?"

Our job – as true **purpose-driven innovators** – is to <u>carefully</u>, <u>thoroughly</u>, and <u>conscientiously</u> consider **all of our actions** – both in <u>operating a business</u>, **and** in <u>producing new artifacts</u> from that business for eventual consumption. This is a practice generally known as *Responsible Innovation.*[67]

Indeed, in everything we do – whether we are the long-time Chairman of the Board of Directors, or the most junior clerk on Day 1 of Job 1 – our job is to ask **new questions** that we have never before been asking ourselves – questions about the ultimate **impacts** of our <u>decisions</u> and <u>actions</u> on the world.

Questions such as...

- Will these decisions and actions make the world – on the whole – a <u>better place</u> than it was before?
- Are we doing <u>more good than harm</u>?
- Are we considering the *impacts* of our decisions and actions on <u>all stakeholders</u> – especially those who are traditionally marginalized because they have no voice in the world of industry (which includes the environment)?
- Are we truly considering 'the other side of growth', so that when we leave this world, we will leave it a better place for <u>subsequent generations</u> than the world that we found?

It is **our job** to <u>ask</u> – and honestly <u>answer</u> – these questions, and then to be **comfortable enough** with the answers that we can <u>get up again tomorrow</u> and do the same thing <u>all over again</u>.

It is **also our job** – should we find that we are <u>not comfortable</u> with the answers to these question on account of others around us over whom we have insufficient influence – to <u>speak truth to power</u>, to <u>blow whistles</u>, and, if need be, to find <u>somewhere else</u> to add value in the world.

It is only through such <u>brave</u> and <u>bold</u> *questioning*, *decision-making*, and *actions* that we will ultimately leave a **legacy** of **true innovation** that we are proud to pass on to those who come after us.

Who Else is Joining Us in This Task?

Fortunately, for us, we are <u>not alone</u>. There is a <u>rapidly growing community</u> all around us – literally thousands upon thousands of conscientious business leaders from all over the world – who are joining us in this sea change of *perspective* and *culture*.

While I do not portend to know *every* organization or group engaged in some aspect of this mission, I do know a few. The following is a list (alphabetized) of a small handful of likeminded organizations that I do know. Undoubtedly – and thankfully – there are countless more yet.

- 1% For The Planet – www.onepercentfortheplanet.org
- 350.org – www.350.org
- 4TU.Centre for Ethics and Technology – www.ethicsandtechnology.eu
- Arab Forum for Environment and Development – www.afedonline.org
- Asia Pacific Adaptation Network – www.asiapacificadapt.net
- Aspen Network of Development Entrepreneurs – www.andeglobal.org
- Business for Social Responsibility – www.bsr.org
- Buckminster Fuller Institute – www.bfi.org
- C40 Cities – www.c40.org
- Caribbean Community Climate Change Center – www.caribbeanclimate.bz
- Center for Humane Technology – www.humanetech.com
- Citizens' Climate Lobby – www.citizensclimatelobby.org
- Climate Action Network International – www.climatenetwork.org
- Climate Cardinals – www.climatecardinals.org
- Climate Justice Alliance – www.climatejusticealliance.org
- Climate Neutral – www.climateneutral.org
- Conscious Capitalism, Inc. – www.consciouscapitalism.org
- Corporate Knights – www.corporateknights.com
- Deep Blue Institute – www.deepblue.institute
- Earthjustice – www.earthjustice.org
- Emerging Markets Private Equity Association (EMPEA) – www.empea.org

- Environmental Defense Fund – www.edf.org
- Environmental Working Group – www.ewg.org
- Ethical OS – www.ethicalos.org
- Extinction Rebellion – www.rebellion.global
- Food Tank – www.foodtank.com
- Fridays for Future – www.fridaysforfuture.org
- Friends of the Earth – www.foe.org
- GatherLab – www.gatherlab.net
- Global Impact Investing Network – www.thegiin.org
- Global Innovation Institute – www.gini.org
- GOGLA – www.gogla.org
- Greenpeace International – www.greenpeace.org
- Health and Environment Alliance – www.env-health.org
- Impact Entrepreneur – impactalchemist.com
- Indigenous Environmental Network – www.ienearth.org
- Julie's Bicycle – www.juliesbicycle.com
- Katerva – www.katerva.org
- La Via Campesina – www.viacampesina.org
- Natural Resources Defense Council – www.nrdc.org
- Naturefriends International – www.nf-int.org
- NESTA – www.nesta.org.uk
- Noah Regen – www.noah.blue
- Oceanic Global – www.oceanic.global
- Omidyar Network – www.omidyar.com
- One Island Institute – www.oneislandinstitute.org
- Organization for Economic Cooperation and Development – www.oecd.org
- Our Kids' Climate – www.ourkidsclimate.org
- Project Drawdown – www.drawdown.org
- PYMWYMIC – www.pymwymic.com

- Rainforest Action Network – www.ran.org

- Shell Foundation – www.shellfoundation.org

- Sunrise Movement – www.sunrisemovement.org

- The Biomimicry Institute – www.biomimicry.org

- The Case Foundation – www.casefoundation.org

- The Climate Collaborative – www.climatecollaborative.com

- The Climate Group – www.theclimategroup.org

- The Climate Leadership Council – www.clcouncil.org

- The Climate Trust – www.climatetrust.org

- The ImPact – www.theimpact.org

- The Mozilla Foundation – www.foundation.mozilla.org

- The New Climate Economy – www.newclimateeconomy.report

- Toniic – www.toniic.com

- Union of Concerned Scientists – www.ucsusa.org

- United States Climate Alliance – www.usclimatealliance.org

- US Aid Global Development Lab – www.usaid.gov/GlobalDevLab

- World Economic Forum (WEF) – www.weforum.org

- World Wildlife Fund – www.worldwildlife.org

Please join with me in thanking all of these wonderful organizations for their tireless efforts in helping us all to see 'the other side of growth'.

End Notes

1 "The Soul of Man Under Socialism", Oscar Wilde, 1891.
   https://www.amazon.com/Soul-Man-Under-Socialism/dp/1717968139/.

2 "About B Corps", B Lab, https://bcorporation.net/about-b-corps.

3 Ibid.

4 Ibid.

5 Ibid.

6 "The B Economy", B Lab, https://bcorporation.net/b-economy.

7 "Standards and Governance", B Lab,
   https://bcorporation.net/about-b-lab/standards-and-governance.

8 "Controversial Issues", B Lab, https://bcorporation.net/controversial-issues.

9 "Remaining Awake Through a Great Revolution", Dr. Martin Luther King, Jr.,
   The Martin Luther King, Jr. Research and Education Institute, Stanford University,
   https://kinginstitute.stanford.edu/king-papers/publications/knock-midnight-
   inspiration-great-sermons-reverend-martin-luther-king-jr-10.

10 "Of Justice and the Conscience", Ten Sermons of Religion, Theodore Parker,
   Crosby, Nichols and Company, Boston, 1852, https://www.amazon.com/Ten-
   Sermons-Religions-Theodore-Parker/dp/1167129830/.

11 Wikipedia entry on *Psalm 24*,
   https://en.wikipedia.org/wiki/Psalm_24.

12 "The Paris Agreement", United Nations Framework Convention on Climate Change,
   https://unfccc.int/process-and-meetings/the-paris-agreement/the-paris-agreement.

13 Wikipedia entry on *2015 United Nations Climate Change Conference*,
   https://en.wikipedia.org/wiki/2015_United_Nations_Climate_Change_Conference.

14 Wikipedia entry on *Paris Agreement*,
   https://en.wikipedia.org/wiki/Paris_Agreement.

15 Ibid.

16 Ibid.

17 Ibid.

18 "We may have just seen the world's highest recorded temperature ever.
   Has that sunk in?", Bob Henson, *The Guardian*, 19 August 2020,
   https://www.theguardian.com/environment/2020/aug/19/highest-recorded-
   temperature-ever-death-valley.

[19] "Global Temperature", *Global Climate Change: Vital Signs of the Planet*, Earth Science Communications Team, NASA Jet Propulsion Laboratory, California Institute of Technology, https://climate.nasa.gov/vital-signs/global-temperature/.

[20] "Interview 29-Year Old Zillionaire Steve Jobs of Apple Computers", *Playboy*, February 1985, Playboy Enterprises.

[21] "Steve Jobs' dent in the universe—the shocking truth revealed!", *Solve/Next Blog*, Solve Next, https://solvenext.com/blog/steve-jobs-dent-in-the-universethe-shocking-truth-revealed.

[22] "Business Roundtable Redefines the Purpose of a Corporation to Promote 'An Economy That Serves All Americans'", Business Roundtable, 19 August 2019, https://www.businessroundtable.org/business-roundtable-redefines-the-purpose-of-a-corporation-to-promote-an-economy-that-serves-all-americans.

[23] "Marc Benioff: We Need a New Capitalism", Marc Benioff, *The New York Times Opinion*, 14 October 2019, https://www.nytimes.com/2019/10/14/opinion/benioff-salesforce-capitalism.html.

[24] Trailblazer: The Power of Business as the Greatest Platform for Change, Marc Benioff, Monica Langley, Random House, 15 October 2019, https://www.amazon.com/Trailblazer-Business-Greatest-Platform-Change/dp/1984825194/.

[25] "Quotes from Climate Bonds 2019 Conference Report: Mobilising Green Trillions, Taxonomies, New financial products, Brown-to-Green transition + More", Leena Fatin, 20 March 2019, Climate Bonds Initiative, https://www.climatebonds.net/2019/03/quotes-climate-bonds-2019-conference-report-mobilising-green-trillions-taxonomies-new.

[26] "Infrastructure Financing Trends", Tomoko Suzuki, Keita Miyaki, Jordan Townswick Pace, *EMCompass Quick Take, Note 5*, April 2016, International Finance Corporation, World Bank Group, http://documents.worldbank.org/curated/en/193791468197952709/pdf/106021-BRI-PUBLIC-EMCompass-5-EMCompass-note05.pdf.

[27] "A Changing World: New trends in emerging market infrastructure finance", Baker McKenzie, 2018, https://www.bakermckenzie.com/en/insight/publications/2018/12/emerging-market-infrastructure-finance.

[28] Ibid.

[29] "Infrastructure Financing Instruments and Incentives", Organization for Economic Co-operation and Development (OECD), 2015, http://www.oecd.org/finance/private-pensions/Infrastructure-Financing-Instruments-and-Incentives.pdf.

30 "Infrastructure Financing Trends", Tomoko Suzuki, Keita Miyaki, Jordan Townswick Pace, *EMCompass Quick Take, Note 5*, April 2016, International Finance Corporation, World Bank Group, http://documents.worldbank.org/curated/en/193791468197952709/pdf/106021-BRI-PUBLIC-EMCompass-5-EMCompass-note05.pdf.

31 "A Changing World: New trends in emerging market infrastructure finance", Baker McKenzie, 2018, https://www.bakermckenzie.com/en/insight/publications/2018/12/emerging-market-infrastructure-finance.

32 "Infrastructure Financing Trends", Tomoko Suzuki, Keita Miyaki, Jordan Townswick Pace, *EMCompass Quick Take, Note 5*, April 2016, International Finance Corporation, World Bank Group, http://documents.worldbank.org/curated/en/193791468197952709/pdf/106021-BRI-PUBLIC-EMCompass-5-EMCompass-note05.pdf.

33 "A Changing World: New trends in emerging market infrastructure finance", Baker McKenzie, 2018, https://www.bakermckenzie.com/en/insight/publications/2018/12/emerging-market-infrastructure-finance.

34 Ibid.

35 "Green bonds: features and trends", *BIS Quarterly Review*, 22 September 2019, BIS, https://www.bis.org/publ/qtrpdf/r_qt1909z.htm.

36 "Red Hot Year for Green Bonds", VanEck Securities Corporation, 02 February 2020, https://www.etftrends.com/tactical-allocation-channel/red-hot-year-for-green-bonds/.

37 "Future Returns: Green Bonds on the Rise", Abby Schultz, 08 October 2019, *Barrons*, https://www.barrons.com/articles/future-returns-green-bonds-on-the-rise-01570541371.

38 "Greening the bond market", Rikkert Scholten, 24 April 2020, *Robeko Insight*, Robeco, https://www.robeco.com/en/insights/2020/04/greening-the-bond-market.html.

39 "Tracking the growth of green bonds", Elaine Tan, 24 July 2019, *Refinitiv Perspectives*, Refinitiv, https://www.refinitiv.com/perspectives/market-insights/tracking-the-growth-of-green-bonds/.

40 "The numbers suggest the green investing 'mega trend' is here to stay", Elliot Smith, 14 February 2020, *CNBC Sustainable Energy*, https://www.cnbc.com/2020/02/14/esg-investing-numbers-suggest-green-investing-mega-trend-is-here.html.

41 Emerging Markets Green Bonds Report 2019, International Finance Corporation, World Bank Group, Spring 2020, https://www.ifc.org/wps/wcm/connect/a64560ef-b074-4a53-8173-f678ccb4f9cd/202005-EM-Green-Bonds-Report-2019.pdf?MOD=AJPERES&CVID=n7Gtahg.

[42] "How the UAE is leading the way for green financing in the GCC", Timucin Engin, Gulf Business, 01 June 2019, https://gulfbusiness.com/uae-leading-way-green-financing-gcc/.

[43] "Apple raises €2bn in green bonds", Patrick Temple-West, *Financial Times*, 07 November 2019, https://www.ft.com/content/918c648c-01ae-11ea-b7bc-f3fa4e77dd47.

[44] "How Apple's $1 Billion Bond Could Help the Planet", Aaron Pressman, *Fortune*, 13 Jun 2017, https://fortune.com/2017/06/13/apple-second-green-bond.

[45] "Ford and Microsoft invest in $1 billion bond for climate projects", Will Nichols, *GreenBiz*, 11 November 2013, https://www.greenbiz.com/article/ford-and-microsoft-invest-1-billion-bond-climate-projects.

[46] "Microsoft Makes First Climate Fund Investment, Joins Green Group", Dina Bass, *Bloomberg Green*, 21 July 2020, https://www.bloomberg.com/news/articles/2020-07-21/microsoft-nike-unilever-announce-global-carbon-neutral-group.

[47] "What Successful Public-Private Partnerships Do", Elyse Maltin, *Harvard Business Review*, 08 January 2019, https://hbr.org/2019/01/what-successful-public-private-partnerships-do.

[48] "The rising advantage of public-private partnerships", Michael Della Rocca, 19 July 2017, McKinsey & Company, https://www.mckinsey.com/industries/capital-projects-and-infrastructure/our-insights/the-rising-advantage-of-public-private-partnerships.

[49] "How Do You Build Effective Public-Private Partnerships?", Isabel Marques De Sá, 16 May 2017, *Yale Insights*, Yale School of Management, https://insights.som.yale.edu/insights/how-do-you-build-effective-public-private-partnerships.

[50] "Public-Private Partnerships Are Popular, But Are They Practical?", Ryan Holeywell, November 2013, *Governing – The Future of States and Localities*, https://www.governing.com/topics/transportation-infrastructure/gov-public-private-popular.html.

[51] "Trends that will drive global PPPs in 2019", David Baxter, 24 January 2019, *World Bank Blog*, World Bank Group, https://blogs.worldbank.org/ppps/trends-will-drive-global-ppps-2019.

[52] "Public-private partnerships in the US: The state of the market and the road ahead", PwC, November 2016, https://www.pwc.com/us/en/capital-projects-infrastructure/publications/assets/pwc-us-public-private-partnerships.pdf.

[53] "New International Survey Reveals Trends in Operational PPP Projects", Service Works Global, 2020, https://www.swg.com/new-survey-reveals-trends-ppp-projects/.

[54] "Public Private Partnership policy in UAE : What you need to know", Atie J El Mouallem, 2018, https://atiejelmouallem.com/public-private-partnership-policy-in-uae/.

[55] Middle East & Africa PPP Guide, Neil Cuthbert, Atif Choudhary, May 2018, Dentons, https://www.dentons.com/-/media/pdfs/guides-reports-and-whitepapers/middle-east-and-africa-ppp-guide.ashx.

[56] "A Changing World: New trends in emerging market infrastructure finance", Baker McKenzie, 2018, https://www.bakermckenzie.com/en/insight/publications/2018/12/emerging-market-infrastructure-finance.

[57] Ibid.

[58] Ibid.

[59] Ibid.

[60] Infrastructure Financing Instruments and Incentives, Organization for Economic Co-operation and Development (OECD), 2015, http://www.oecd.org/finance/private-pensions/Infrastructure-Financing-Instruments-and-Incentives.pdf.

[61] "Infrastructure Financing Trends", Tomoko Suzuki, Keita Miyaki, Jordan Townswick Pace, EMCompass Quick Take, Note 5, April 2016, International Finance Corporation, World Bank Group, http://documents.worldbank.org/curated/en/193791468197952709/pdf/106021-BRI-PUBLIC-EMCompass-5-EMCompass-note05.pdf.

[62] "Tracking the growth of green bonds", Elaine Tan, 24 July 2019, *Refinitiv Perspectives*, Refinitiv, https://www.refinitiv.com/perspectives/market-insights/tracking-the-growth-of-green-bonds/.

[63] Infrastructure Financing Instruments and Incentives, Organization for Economic Co-operation and Development (OECD), 2015, http://www.oecd.org/finance/private-pensions/Infrastructure-Financing-Instruments-and-Incentives.pdf.

[64] Ibid.

[65] "The rising advantage of public-private partnerships", Michael Della Rocca, 19 July 2017, McKinsey & Company, https://www.mckinsey.com/industries/capital-projects-and-infrastructure/our-insights/the-rising-advantage-of-public-private-partnerships.

[66] "What Successful Public-Private Partnerships Do", Elyse Maltin, *Harvard Business Review*, 08 January 2019, https://hbr.org/2019/01/what-successful-public-private-partnerships-do.

[67] "What is responsible innovation, and why should tech giants take it seriously?", James Peckham, *TechRadar*, 27 August 27 2018, https://www.techradar.com/news/what-is-responsible-innovation-and-why-should-tech-giants-take-it-seriously.

Made in the USA
Monee, IL
17 April 2021